Benjamin Franklin

Inventor and Founding Father

Kaitlyn Duling

Cavendish
Square

New York

Published in 2020 by Cavendish Square Publishing, LLC
243 5th Avenue, Suite 136, New York, NY 10016

First Edition

Website: cavendishsq.com

This publication represents the opinions and views of the author based on his or her personal experience, knowledge, and research. The information in this book serves as a general guide only. The author and publisher have used their best efforts in preparing this book and disclaim liability rising directly or indirectly from the use and application of this book.

All websites were available and accurate when this book was sent to press.

Library of Congress Cataloging-in-Publication Data

Names: Duling, Kaitlyn, author.
Title: Benjamin Franklin : inventor and founding father / Kaitlyn Duling.
Description: First edition. | New York : Cavendish Square, [2020] | Series: Great American entrepreneurs | Includes bibliographical references and index. | Audience: Grades 9-12.
Identifiers: LCCN 2018047430 (print) | LCCN 2018048409 (ebook) | ISBN 9781502645388 (ebook) | ISBN 9781502645371 (library bound) | ISBN 9781502645364 (pbk.)
Subjects: LCSH: Franklin, Benjamin, 1706-1790--Juvenile literature. | Statesmen--United States--Biography--Juvenile literature. | Scientists--United States--Biography--Juvenile literature. | Inventors--United States--Biography--Juvenile literature. | Printers--United States--Biography--Juvenile literature.
Classification: LCC E302.6.F8 (ebook) | LCC E302.6.F8 D845 2020 (print) | DDC 973.3092 [B] --dc23
LC record available at https://lccn.loc.gov/2018047430

Editorial Director: David McNamara
Editor: Kristen Susienka
Copy Editor: Alex Tessman
Art Director: Alan Sliwinski
Designer: Joseph Parenteau
Production Coordinator: Karol Szymczuk
Photo Research: J8 Media

The photographs in this book are used by permission and through the courtesy of: Cover John Parrot/Stocktrek Images/Getty Images; p. 4, 64 Everett Historical/Shutterstock.com; p. 6, 8, 35, 38-39, 50-51 Bettman/Getty Images; p. 11 Ann Ronan Pictures/Print Collector/Getty Images; p. 17 Anonymous/Getty Images; p. 20-21 John Trumbull/Wikimedia Commons/File:The Capture of the Hessians at Trenton December 26 1776.jpeg/Public Domain; p. 26 Universal History Archive/Getty Images; p. 30 Swampyank/Wikimedia Commons/File:Old South Meeting House in Boston MA.jpg/Public Domain; p. 41 Natalia Bratslavsky/Shutterstock.com; p. 44 Carolina K. Smith MD/Shutterstock.com; p. 48 John Trumbull/Wikimedia Commons/File:Committee of Five, 1776.png/Public Domain; p. 57 John Wesley Jarvis/Wikimedia Commons/File:Thomas Paine A16220.jpg/Public Domain; p. 62 Mather Brown/Wikimedia Commons/File:WilliamFranklin.jpeg/Public Domain; p. 72 Rainer Lesniewski/Shutterstock.com; p. 74 Vince Flango/Wikimedia Commons/File:Glassarmonica.jpg/Public Domain; p. 78 Stock Montage/Stock Montage/Getty Images; p. 81 Library of Congress/Wikimedia Commons/File:Mark Twain by Abdullah Frères, 1867.jpg/Public Domain; p. 84 © Hulton-Deutsch Collection/CORBIS/Corbis via Getty Images; p. 86-87 Howard Chandler Christy/Wikimedia Commons/File:Scene at the Signing of the Constitution of the United States.jpg/Public Domain; p. 91 Oleksandr Osipov/Shutterstock.com; p. 94 Mira/Alamy Stock Photo; p. 97 Robynrg/Shutterstock.com; p. 99 Library of Congress/Wikimedia Commons/File:US Declaration of Independence draft 1.jpg/Public Domain; p. 100 Kevin Burkett/Wikimedia Commons/File:Ben Franklin Bridge3.jpg/CC BY SA 2.0; p. 103 Fotosearch/Getty Images.

Printed in the United States of America

CONTENTS

Inventor, Diplomat, Founding Father

Benjamin Franklin was born in the midst of many great changes. His life blossomed during a period of political upheaval, scientific discovery, and social evolution. Had he been born into another time and place, his life may have taken a different course. However, for Franklin, the eighteenth century was the perfect opportunity to leave his mark.

Today we remember Franklin for his inventions, scientific experiments, publications, leadership, and, eventually, his role as a Founding Father of the United States. How was he able to do so many things over the course of just a few decades? The answer lies not only in the specific time period but in Franklin's own determination, enthusiasm, and endless pursuit of those things that thrilled him.

This engraving, based on one of Franklin's favorite portraits of himself, highlights the Founding Father's scientific experiments and his successes as an inventor and writer. These were just some of Franklin's many accomplishments.

A World of Possibilities

Benjamin Franklin came of age in Boston, Massachusetts, a bustling port city that was full of possibility. From Boston to Philadelphia, London to France, Franklin made waves across the world. Throughout his life, he moved easily between the Old World and the New World, transferring ideas, passions, and inspirations with him. Though we think of Franklin as a Founding Father of early America, he also spent much time in Europe, often working on behalf of his homeland. Just as Franklin didn't confine his thoughts to things that had already been invented and discovered, neither did he keep himself at home, knowledgeable only of what was happening in the colonies.

Throughout his life, Franklin's endless pursuit of the breadth and depth of knowledge served him well—little did he know that

As a Founding Father, Franklin would be one of fifty-six men who signed the Declaration of Independence on July 4, 1776. The document declared that the thirteen British colonies were completely independent from the kingdom of Great Britain.

one day, we would inherit all he put forth into the world. Today, we are touched by his memory in our day-to-day lives. From strides in electricity and optics, to his input on the Declaration of Independence and the US Constitution, Franklin's thoughts are woven into America's founding documents and earliest innovations. He was moving and shaking with the times socially and politically too: an abolitionist and ardent defender of the freedom of speech, Franklin was not only at the helm of the American Revolution, but he helped to form Americans' most basic and earliest understandings of what it meant to be an American. US history and values have been shaped by Franklin's thoughts and actions, just as they were molded by many other Founding Fathers.

A Man of Many Skills

Benjamin Franklin's story is so particularly powerful because he didn't simply work on the Declaration of Independence. He didn't only invent bifocals. His almanac wasn't his crowning achievement. No, Franklin's life must be viewed from a macro level—nothing he dreamed or achieved was done outside of that prime historical moment in which he lived, and none of it was completed in a vacuum. His thoughts, projects, experiments, and writings were all completed in relation to one another. Without each of his life experiences, there would never have been a *next* experience or achievement.

Franklin's legacy has been honored in countless ways, including the placement of his portrait on the $100 bill. He has also become part of our collective memory, as an inventor, a diplomat, and an inextricable part of America's founding story. Without him, the United States might be a very different place.

CHAPTER ONE

An American Revolution

Born in 1706, Benjamin Franklin was not the legal resident of a state but was born, instead, into an American colony. The colonies were run by the country of England, situated across the Atlantic Ocean. The colonies were a diverse amalgamation of immigrants from various European locales, as well as slaves forced from their own homelands and transported to the colonies from Africa. The 1700s saw great changes for the colonies, as well as in England and France. The transformation of North America's eastern coast would happen both slowly and deliberately, but also relatively suddenly, in a century-long burst of social, political, and scientific innovation.

The thirteen original colonies, some of which have kept similar shapes and sizes as states, were situated on the eastern edge of central North America.

The Thirteen Original Colonies

The settlement and control of the Americas by European powers took place over hundreds of years. Between the 1400s and 1600s, Spaniards, French explorers, and leaders from other European countries all deliberately took control of various parts of South and North America. Originally, the British colonies were settled by British immigrants in the 1600s. After traveling by boat from England, they arrived on land that was occupied by Native American tribes. They saw this new world as a place of untouched opportunity—full of resources, land, adventure, and wealth that had yet to be claimed. Through a combination of military force, the spread of disease, and population growth, the colonists were able to take control of the land and wrest it away from its previous Native inhabitants. This happened in the early 1600s, about one hundred years before Benjamin Franklin's birth.

Benjamin Franklin was born in Boston, part of the Massachusetts Bay Colony. This colony was established in the 1620s by Puritans and was home to a harbor that would eventually become a lucrative point of trade, travel, and conflict. The Puritans desired to create a new church in the New World.

Even though those living in Massachusetts Bay and other colonies did things like start churches, run businesses, and raise families, their ruling government was in England. They followed the laws of England and paid taxes to England. Though they were under British rule and often felt frustrated by that fact, those living in the British colonies also benefited economically from that relationship. The thirteen original colonies (Delaware, Pennsylvania, New Jersey, Georgia, Connecticut, Massachusetts Bay, Maryland, South Carolina, New Hampshire, Virginia, New York, North Carolina, and Rhode Island and Providence

Plantations) benefited from England's global trading power. The New World was full of natural resources, such as fur, animal skins, wood, and tobacco.

Slavery in Colonial America

As economic conditions in the colonies grew prosperous, slave plantations and the slave trade became bedrock, foundational suppliers of that prosperity. Between 1600 and 1750, the population of slaves in the British colonies grew exponentially. By 1700, there were twenty-five thousand slaves in the colonies.

In colonial and early America, slaves did various types of work, including planting, harvesting, drying, and rolling tobacco, an extremely profitable crop in the South.

By 1750, Virginia alone had one hundred thousand slaves. By 1790, slaves would make up about 34 percent of the total population of the United States.[1]

Slavery was practiced in every colony, and it was woven deeply into the economic and social structures of the Southern colonies in particular. It did not evolve randomly. In 1670, slavery was formally established and recognized by the Virginia House of Burgesses, though servants and slaves had been present in North America for many decades already. The law declared, "All servants not being Christians imported into this colony by shipping shall be slaves for their lives."[2] Tobacco, rice, and indigo were all produced by slave labor. These were major export crops for many Southern colonies.

This was the world that Benjamin Franklin was born into— one in which white men collectively held freedom and power and built the early economy on the backs of those imported into their country and forced into labor. Over the course of the Atlantic slave trade, an estimated twelve million slaves were transported from Africa to the Americas.

Steps Toward Revolution

Life in the colonies was not always peaceful. Conflicts arose between Spain, Britain, and France. They played out in battles and wars waged up and down North and South America. The main European conflict truly came to a head in 1754, with the dawn of the French and Indian War. The name of this war can be somewhat misleading, as it was actually a conflict between Britain and France. It was fought on North American soil, as British soldiers and colonists clashed with French forces and those Native American forces that chose to ally with France. At times, the British contingent was also supported

BENJAMIN FRANKLIN, FREEMASON

In the 1730s, Benjamin Franklin was initiated into St. John's Lodge, a Masonic lodge in Philadelphia, Pennsylvania. Freemasonry is a group of fraternal organizations whose histories trace back to fourteenth-century stonemasons. Members of Masonic lodges, which operate independently, are known as Freemasons. The lodges conduct business, rituals, and social events. Their charities contribute to various fields.

Franklin was very active in Freemasonry, holding leadership positions and often speaking highly of the organization. He eventually became the Grand Master of Pennsylvania and was very active in French Freemasonry. In a 1738 letter to his mother, Franklin wrote, "Freemasons have no principles or practices that are inconsistent with religion and good manners."[3]

Though they were originally founded and run in line with genteel, English behavior, the Freemasons ultimately took on a leading role in the American Revolution. George Washington, Alexander Hamilton, and John Hancock were fellow members. Together with other leaders, they used the Masonic lodges as convenient gathering places for revolutionary discussions and plans.

by various tribes. Some historians refer to this war as the Seven Years' War, which encompasses fighting that took place on five continents.

The French and Indian War caused colonial men to travel significant distances across the colonies, encountering people and places that they may not have otherwise seen, and it brought those living in the colonies together under a common cause. At that time, Benjamin Franklin even formed a plan to create a unified government, called the Albany Plan of the Union, that would help coordinate defense across the colonies, but his idea was ultimately rejected by both the colonial delegates and British representatives. The British were not keen to consolidate power in the colonies, and colonists were wary of a unified, taxing body.

The most salient point on the subject of the French and Indian War as it relates to the eventual Revolutionary War is that it was, in a word, *expensive*. It is estimated that the war cost the British treasury 70,000,000 pounds (over $1.8 trillion in 2018).

Following the war, the British had huge debts to repay. In order to help minimize their debt, British leaders increased taxation on the colonies. New taxes on sugar, stamps, and other materials sowed discontent in the thirteen colonies. The Stamp Act of 1765 caused particular ire. This was not a tax on postage stamps, like we might imagine a stamp tax would be today. It actually required all printed materials in the colonies to be printed on special stamped paper that was produced in London. This paper included an embossed label that proved the tax had been paid. Legal documents, newspapers, magazines, and even playing cards were subject to this new rule. According to British leaders, the tax paid for British soldiers stationed in North America after the French and Indian War.

Benjamin Franklin protested heavily against the Stamp Act. In testimony recorded in 1766, while he was living and working in London, he said, "The frontier counties, all along the continent, having been frequently ravaged by the enemy and greatly impoverished, are able to pay very little tax … In my opinion there is not gold and silver enough in the colonies to pay the stamp duty for one year."[4]

It was around this time that colonists began to utilize the phrase "no taxation without representation," which spoke to the fact that colonists were taxed even though they had no representatives in Parliament, Britain's ruling body, and did not have any formal input when it came to making laws about their own land.

In a question-and-answer period during the 1766 testimony, Franklin was asked about the Stamp Act and the colonists' attitudes toward England in general. Speaking of colonists' frustration and loss of respect for England, he said:

> Q. If the act is not repealed, what do you think will be the consequences?
>
> A. A total loss of the respect and affection the people of America bear to this country, and of all the commerce that depends on that respect and affection.
>
> Q. If the Stamp Act should be repealed, would it induce the assemblies of America to acknowledge the right of Parliament to tax them, and would they erase their resolutions [against the Stamp Act]?
>
> A. No, never.
>
> Q. Is there no means of obliging them to erase those resolutions?
>
> A. None that I know of; they will never do it, unless compelled by force of arms.

Q. Is there a power on earth that can force them to erase them?

A. No power, how greatsoever, can force men to change their opinions …

Q. What used to be the pride of the Americans?

A. To indulge in the fashions and manufactures of Great Britain.

Q. What is now their pride?

A. To wear their old clothes over again, till they can make new ones.[5]

In this short question-and-answer period, Franklin was giving a warning to Parliament and the people of England: the colonists would not back down about the Stamp Act unless "compelled by force of arms," or pushed to the brink of war. In the last question of pride, Franklin asserts that Americans are finished making purchases from England. They would wear the same clothes over and over again, until they could produce their own and become self-sustaining. This exchange acted as but a small preview of the revolution that was soon to come.

Sipping Tea in the Colonies

As the mid-1700s carried on, Parliament continued to enact duties on various supplies, including paper, glass, and tea. The trade regulations were executed by the Board of Customs, a body situated in Boston, Franklin's home city. As more taxes were enacted, the colonists' frustration began to grow.

On March 5, 1770, a large crowd surrounded a group of British soldiers and began to threaten them, throwing rocks and debris. One soldier fell to the ground after being clubbed, prompting the other soldiers to fire into the crowd. Eleven

The Boston Tea Party was a raucous event that involved demonstrators destroying an entire shipment of tea imported by the East India Company.

colonists were hit by bullets, and five lost their lives. This incident would come to be known as the Boston Massacre, and it helped to sow even more seeds of distrust and negative sentiment against the British.

In May 1773, Parliament passed the Tea Act, which would come to be one of the defining decisions that led to the American Revolution. The act sought to help the British East India Company, a struggling industry leader with an excess of tea, undersell tea that was then being imported from the Dutch. In essence, it hoped to defy colonial smugglers and merchants, rigging the market in favor of the East India Company. On December 16, a group known as the Sons of Liberty disguised themselves as Native Americans, boarded three ships owned by the East India Company, and threw chests of tea overboard into Boston Harbor. They ended up destroying an entire shipment of tea and sparking what would eventually be the run-up to the Revolutionary War. An account of the "dumping" was printed in the *Boston Gazette* on December 20, 1773:

> On Tuesday last the body of the people of this and all the adjacent towns, and others from the distance of twenty miles [32 kilometers], assembled at the old south meeting-house, to inquire the reason of the delay in sending the ship Dartmouth, with the East-India Tea back to London; and having found that the owner had not taken the necessary steps for that purpose, they enjoin'd him at his peril to demand of the collector of the customs a clearance for the ship, and appointed a committee of ten to see it perform'd; after which they adjourn'd to the Thursday following ten o'clock ... The people finding all their efforts to preserve the property of the East India company and return it safely to London, frustrated by the tea consignees, the collector of the customs and the governor of the province, DISSOLVED their meeting.—But, BEHOLD what followed! A number of brave and resolute men, determined to do all in their power to save their country from the ruin which their enemies had plotted, in less than four hours, emptied every chest of tea on board the three ships commanded by captains Hall, Bruce, and Coffin, amounting to 342 chests, into the sea ! ! without the least damage done to the ships or any other property. The masters and owners are

well pleas'd that their ships are thus clear'd; and the people are almost universally congratulating each other on this happy event.[6]

While the *Boston Gazette* reported that the people were "almost universally congratulating each other," the one group that was not at all happy about the incident was the British government. This act of defiance set off a blaze of negative relations that had begun to burn years beforehand. With active rebellions like these, the colonists were solidly on the path to eventual war.

Headed for War

Just two months later, the Massachusetts Bay Colony was declared in a state of rebellion. Reactions to the Boston Tea Party, as the incident was called, were mixed—some colonists wanted to repay the debts from the event and figure out how to live peacefully under British rule. Others lived in a state of constant unrest and wished to be out from under the British flag. The discussions coalesced into the First Continental Congress, a meeting in Philadelphia in 1774 that brought together twelve of the colonies. Georgia did not attend the Congress, as they were in the midst of a Native American uprising and needed to use British funds for military supplies.

The official role of the Congress was to organize resistance to the Coercive Acts, also known as the Intolerable Acts. These were four acts established by Parliament that aimed to restore order in the Massachusetts Bay Colony and punish those involved in the Boston Tea Party. The acts closed the port of Boston until damages were paid; restricted Massachusetts's government; restricted the ability of those in Massachusetts

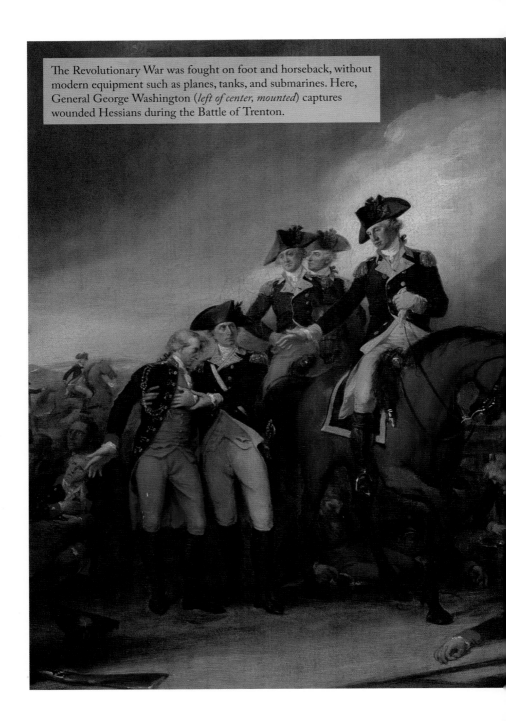

The Revolutionary War was fought on foot and horseback, without modern equipment such as planes, tanks, and submarines. Here, General George Washington (*left of center, mounted*) captures wounded Hessians during the Battle of Trenton.

to prosecute British officials; and required colonists to house British troops, including in their private homes, on demand. It also extended freedom of worship to Catholics in Canada, which was not met with positive feelings from the majority-Protestant colonists.

In response to these acts, the First Continental Congress, of which Benjamin Franklin was a part, decided that the only allegiance the colonists owed to Britain was to the king. They would no longer recognize Parliament's right to pass legislation related to the colonies. It was around this time that the colonies became divided into two camps: Loyalists, who supported British rule, and Patriots, who opposed it.

In the spring of 1775, the colonists had had enough. At that time, the Continental Congress became an official national government. An army was raised in order to fight the British, and George Washington, who had gained experience as an officer in the French and Indian War, was put at the helm. The colonies began to print their own money. British soldiers were pushed out of Boston. In July 1776, the Declaration of Independence was drafted, most notably by Thomas Jefferson, but with much input from other Founding Fathers, including Benjamin Franklin. It was unanimously adopted on July 4, 1776, granting that each of the colonies was now independent.

The armed conflict between the colonies and Great Britain would continue through 1783. During this time, France became one of America's most important allies. Without French support, America may well have lost the war. Throughout the years, the Continental Congress struggled to fund its Continental Army and relied on contributions from the various states, rather than taxes or another formal fundraising venture.

By 1783, the fledgling country negotiated the Treaty of Paris, which officially ended the Revolutionary War. Franklin helped to draft this document, ensuring that the United States was recognized as independent and could claim nearly all the territory south of Canada and east of the Mississippi River.

In the years immediately following the war, the young nation would be met with difficult financial situations, rivalries between states, and other domestic issues. The Articles of Confederation, America's first constitution, were proven to be insufficient. Franklin, among many others, helped to draft the new US Constitution in 1787. From then on, the country would be governed by the US Congress and the president, and the Constitution would become the founding document on which the laws of the United States would be based.

Industrial Revolution and Other Advances

While Benjamin Franklin witnessed great political and social upheaval in his lifetime, he also experienced eras of serious technological advancement, most prominently the Industrial Revolution. This major turning point in history began in Great Britain around 1760, but quickly spread to the British colonies and grew in both size and scope. Before the Industrial Revolution, most items were produced by hand. During this revolution, machines became king. Not only were entire economies changed and grown in massive ways, but day-to-day life was greatly affected.

The main industries involved in the Industrial Revolution were textiles and iron, both aided by the creation of the steam engine. Factories and mass production became the norm, and societies began to shift from a largely rural, agrarian lifestyle to one focused on urban, industrial life and manufacturing. This time period also saw the creation of the stock exchange and the founding of modern economics. Scottish social philosopher

Adam Smith published his *Wealth of Nations* in 1776, which would change ideas surrounding free enterprise, private ownership, and government interference in the marketplace. Though Smith supported free trade and capitalism, he also concerned himself with the natural outcomes of this type of capitalist society. He wrote of inequality, "Wherever there is great property there is great inequality. For one very rich man there must be at least five hundred poor, and the affluence of the few supposes the indigence of the many. The affluence of the rich excites the indignation of the poor, who are often both driven by want, and prompted by envy, to invade his possessions."[7]

The 1700s were a time of change on many fronts— economic, industrial, political, social. But when it comes to the history of communication, scant contributions were made. Movable type and the printing press were introduced in the 1300s and 1400s, respectively. The biggest eighteenth-century advancement was the 1792 creation of the semaphore telegraph system by Claude Chappe, a Frenchman. Chappe's system covered France with over five hundred stations, between which messages could be communicated, often about the French Revolution. The system included a semaphore shape for each letter of the alphabet. Two to three symbols per minute were transferred using rods and panels.

Tumultuous Times

In the postwar years, and even during the Revolutionary War, Franklin had grown to be an old man. Born into a peaceful colony, he experienced decades of tumultuous change in North America's evolving coastal cities: The complicated, painful birth of a new nation out of the ashes of armed conflict with its ruling crown. An evolving economic and industrial landscape. All of these situations came together to create a bustling century that had innovation and revolution at its center. The time was ripe for new inventions, daring experiments, careful diplomacy, and new forms of communication. The son of a candlemaker, Franklin matured and learned throughout his life, until he was ready to help light and fan the flames of freedom as they ignited in his own birth city, colony of origin, and eventually, the new nation that he would also call "home."

CHAPTER TWO

The Busy Life of Benjamin Franklin

Benjamin Franklin achieved countless things in his lifetime, but none of those events came to fruition without a background. No individual can be divorced from his or her past, and Franklin is the same. His childhood and younger years were the foundation on which he built a life of innovation and adventure.

Franklin's Early Years

Franklin was born in 1706. Today, we celebrate his birthday on January 17, but that wasn't always the recognized day of his birth. Until 1752, Great Britain used the Julian calendar, which put Franklin's birthdate on January 6. When the country switched to the Gregorian calendar,

Though Franklin had a notable professional career, he also maintained a busy home life, marrying and raising children amid his travels. This image shows him and his wife, Deborah, at the kitchen table.

which is what we still use today, the day was moved eleven days ahead. Writing to his wife, Deborah Franklin, in 1773, Franklin said, "I feel still some Regard for this Sixth of January, as my old nominal Birth-day."[1] However, in colonial America, birthdays weren't heavily celebrated. Most years, Franklin would treat the day just like any other.

We do know for a fact that Franklin was born on a Sunday in Boston, Massachusetts. His birthplace is located at 17 Milk Street. At the time, Boston was less of a city and more like a large town, with a population of about seven thousand. His father, Josiah Franklin, was an immigrant from Northamptonshire, England. Josiah traveled to the colonies in 1682, where he met his second wife, Abiah Folger. Abiah was originally from Nantuket, Massachusetts. Josiah, who was a candle- and soap maker by trade, and Abiah would eventually come to be the parents of seventeen children. Josiah had had seven children with his first wife, Anne Child. Anne passed away in 1689, and Josiah quickly married Abiah Folger. Abiah bore ten children total. Benjamin Franklin was Josiah's fifteenth child, and he was the youngest son of the family.

Josiah sent his son to the city's grammar school when he was eight years old. After less than a year at grammar school, Franklin transferred to the more affordable Mr. George Brownell's school for writing and arithmetic. It was a boarding school, so Franklin lived there instead of in the small, crowded house with his large family. Franklin wrote in his autobiography of the school: "My father … sent me to a school for writing and arithmetic, kept by a then famous man, George Brownell, very successful in his profession generally, and that by mild, encouraging methods. Under him I acquired fair writing pretty soon … but I failed in the arithmetic, and made no progress in it."[2]

Franklin loved to read and write. In fact, reading was his favorite pastime. Schooling encouraged his reading and writing skills, and Franklin was soon collecting all sorts of books. A lover of the sea, he taught himself how to swim from *The Art of Swimming*, a book! His home was very close to Boston Harbor, so Franklin could see the ships coming and going each day. He desperately wanted to be a sailor, adventuring on the open sea. But his father did not approve of this plan. Franklin's older brother Josiah had gone to sea on a trading vessel and never returned. The emotional pain from that loss plagued the elder Josiah Franklin. It was his desire that young Ben become a preacher. Benjamin Franklin had been baptized on the day he was born at Old South Church's Cedar Meeting House, located on Washington Street in Boston. Many members of his family were prominent leaders in the church, which would also count Phillis Wheatley, Samuel Adams, and William Dawes as members.

By the time he turned ten years old, Franklin's family could no longer afford formal education for their son. He was forced to drop out of school and put his dreams of ministry and sailing behind him. This early end to formal education wasn't unheard of for youth of the time period. He moved into work at his father's soap and candle shop. The work was smelly and boring, and Franklin still daydreamed of sailing away on one of the ships in Boston Harbor. Later, he would describe the work as time spent "cutting wick for the candles, filling the dipping mold and the molds for cast candles, attending the shop, going on errands, etc."[3]

Even though he worked daily in the shop, Franklin remained dedicated to books and learning. His father, too, knew that his son wouldn't work in the shop forever. He often brought him out around the city to view different occupations, hopeful that Franklin would find something suitable that was *not* at sea.

Today, you can still visit the Old South Church Meeting House where Benjamin Franklin was baptized. It has survived through Boston's modern-day periods of growth and change.

Eventually, one of those trips led them to Franklin's brother's print shop. Twenty-one-year-old James had recently returned from London, where he learned how to print. The labor was hard and not held in very high esteem. Printers carted around heavy trays of type, pounded them with wooden mallets, and pressed everything manually. The Industrial Revolution had not yet come to Boston. Most of the work was still done by hand. At age twelve, Franklin began to apprentice in James's new shop.

Starting in 1721, James ran a newspaper, called the *New England Courant*, out of his print shop. Boston only had two other papers at the time, the *Boston News-Letter* and the *Boston Gazette*. For his publication, James hoped to have a unique, feisty voice that picked fights with the local establishment. It included stories, essays, poems, and all sorts of news. Franklin was immediately interested in writing for the paper, but his brother refused to allow it. In a fit of creative ingenuity, Franklin created a character—Silence Dogood—who was a country widow that wrote witty letters. He slipped the first of the letters under his brother's print shop door in the middle of the night. James had no idea who Silence Dogood was, but he thought her letters were funny and wise enough for his paper. He published the first one on April 2, 1722. The second letter, published on April 16, reads in part:

> I shall conclude this with my own Character, which (one would think) I should be best able to give. *Know then*, That I am an Enemy to Vice, and a Friend to Vertue. I am one of an extensive Charity, and a great Forgiver of *private* Injuries: A hearty Lover of the Clergy and all good Men, and a mortal Enemy to arbitrary Government and unlimited Power. I am

naturally very jealous for the Rights and Liberties of my Country; and the least appearance of an Incroachment on those invaluable Priviledges, is apt to make my Blood boil exceedingly. I have likewise a natural Inclination to observe and reprove the Faults of others, at which I have an excellent Faculty. I speak this by Way of Warning to all such whose Offences shall come under my Cognizance, for I never intend to wrap my Talent in a Napkin. To be brief; I am courteous and affable, good humour'd (unless I am first provok'd,) and handsome, and sometimes witty, but always, Sir, Your Friend and Humble Servant,

Silence Dogood[4]

The Silence Dogood letters proved to be immensely popular. There would be fourteen letters in total, stretching from April to October. By fall, James began to suspect the true author of the letters. He was *not* happy with Benjamin. After he confronted Franklin about the letters, the two brothers began to fight quite often. Franklin was supposed to apprentice at the shop until he was twenty-one years old, but the unhappy conditions pushed him to run away at age seventeen.

Philadelphia

Franklin didn't just want to find another job in Boston. He wanted to get out of town. He sold some of his books to purchase a ship ticket out of Boston Harbor. The boat took him first to New York City, following a journey of three days and nearly 300 miles (483 km). Once there, he sought out the advice of William Bradford, New York City's only printer.

Bradford advised him to continue south to Philadelphia. Franklin agreed, and took the six-day trip around the coast of New Jersey by ship. At the end of the ride, he hiked 50 miles (81 km) across New Jersey on foot, and then took to the Delaware River by rowboat.

In his autobiography, Franklin describes his arrival in Philadelphia in October 1723, finally finished with the arduous journey. He was dirty, wearing workman's clothes, with very few coins in his pocket. He describes wandering up Market Street:

> Then I walked up the street, gazing about till near the market-house I met a boy with bread. I had made many a meal on bread, and, inquiring where he got it, I went immediately to the baker's he directed me to, in Secondstreet, and ask'd for bisket, intending such as we had in Boston; but they, it seems, were not made in Philadelphia. Then I asked for a three-penny loaf, and was told they had none such. So not considering or knowing the difference of money, and the greater cheapness nor the names of his bread, I made him give me three-penny worth of any sort. He gave me, accordingly, three great puffy rolls. I was surpriz'd at the quantity, but took it, and, having no room in my pockets, walk'd off with a roll under each arm, and eating the other. Thus I went up Market-street as far as Fourth-street, passing by the door of Mr. Read, my future wife's father; when she, standing at the door, saw me, and thought I made, as I certainly did, a most awkward, ridiculous appearance.[5]

Once he was firmly settled in Philadelphia, Franklin managed to build on his apprenticeship to secure a job in Samuel Keimer's print shop. He quickly made friends and developed a social circle. Keimer introduced him to John Read, with whom he was able to find lodging ... and to spend time courting Read's fifteen-year-old daughter, Deborah. Deborah Read was born to John Read and his wife Sarah White Read. Very little is known about her childhood, aside from the fact that she was the second of seven children and received very little formal education.

As it turned out, the Pennsylvania government frequently worked with Bradford and Keimer, so it wasn't long before Governor William Keith heard about the bright and hardworking teenager who was finding success in Keimer's shop. One day, he appeared at the shop and introduced himself to Franklin. The governor offered to help Franklin establish his very own printing shop if Josiah Franklin would agree to invest financially in the project, especially if Keith promised to send Franklin a steady stream of printing orders.

Franklin returned to Boston just seven months after his arrival in Philadelphia, in an effort to persuade his father, but nothing came of it. Josiah was of the opinion that his youngest son was still too young and inexperienced for such a venture.

Back in Philadelphia, Governor Keith offered to put up the money himself, and suggested that Franklin travel to London, England, in order to choose a printing press, type, and other equipment, as well as to meet up with some English booksellers and stationers. The governor supplied a line of credit for the journey. During this time, Deborah and Franklin had become close, and she began to suggest that they get married. However, Franklin was unsure, so he set off for England.

This woodcut, created in the mid-nineteenth century, shows a young Benjamin
Franklin working as an apprentice printer. The printing technology of the day was very
rudimentary, and nearly all parts of the process had to be completed by hand.

London

The journey from Philadelphia to London took seven weeks. Franklin arrived on Christmas Eve 1724. London was much larger than any city Franklin had inhabited thus far. When he arrived, he had received no letters or credit from the governor. Keith was, unfortunately, a very spontaneous person who didn't often keep his promises. Franklin made the best of the situation, though, finding cheap lodging and work at a large printing house called Palmer's. He spent time in coffeehouses and taverns, making friends, engaging with women, and learning about printing and writing along the way.

It was during this eighteen-month stint in London that Franklin published his first essay, a philosophical pamphlet entitled *A Dissertation on Liberty and Necessity, Pleasure and Pain*. In the pamphlet, Franklin laid out a structured argument for the existence of fate and a benevolent God. Only one hundred copies were printed, and Franklin would eventually refute many of the arguments it contained, but it did give him experience in writing philosophical arguments and engaging with complicated ideas. He would utilize these skills throughout his life, especially in his role as a Founding Father.

Franklin set sail back to Philadelphia in July 1726. While on the voyage home, he wrote up a "Plan of Conduct" for himself that he hoped to follow when he arrived back in the colonies. It read:

1. It is necessary for me to be extremely frugal for some time, till I have paid what I owe.
2. To endeavour to speak truth in every instance; to give nobody expectations that are not likely to be answered, but aim at sincerity in every

word and action—the most amiable excellence in a rational being.

3. To apply myself industriously to whatever business I take in hand, and not divert my mind from my business by any foolish project of growing suddenly rich; for industry and patience are the surest means of plenty.

4. I resolve to speak ill of no man whatever, not even in a matter of truth; but rather by some means excuse the faults I hear charged upon others, and upon proper occasions speak all the good I know of every body.[6]

Finding His Footing

By the age of twenty-four, Franklin was ready to open his own print shop. He earned a reputation as a skilled printer and continued to enjoy a freewheeling social life, inviting bright young people over each Friday evening to talk, drink, sing, and think about the issues of the day. Calling themselves the Junto (conference), the group debated and discussed topics of the moral, political, and philosophical realms.

By his mid-twenties, Franklin was interested in settling down and having a family of his own. Though Deborah Read had married a potter named John Rogers while Franklin was away in London, her marriage to him had dissolved as some knowledge came to light—Rogers was rumored to have a wife he had abandoned in England, he was running up debt, and eventually he deserted Deborah and ran off to the West Indies. However, none of these events were grounds for divorce. Eventually, rumors reached Philadelphia that Rogers had died.

At the age of twenty-four, Franklin struck out on his own to open an independent printing shop. No longer an apprentice, Franklin was in charge of his own business. This illustrations shows what the shop might have looked like.

Amidst all of this drama, Franklin and Deborah settled on a common-law marriage. They moved in together in 1730 and never ended up formally marrying. Their nontraditional family structure would become even more complicated when, a few months after they moved in together, Franklin brought home a baby that he had fathered by another woman. He never revealed the name of the other woman, but he assumed sole custody of the boy and named him William. In 1732, Deborah gave birth to her own son, Francis. Sadly, Francis would die just four years later, of smallpox. Years later, she would give birth to a little girl, Sarah, who would be called Sally and would remain close to her father into his old age.

While working at his press, Franklin purchased a weekly newspaper, the *Pennsylvania Gazette*. He turned the paper into the leading publication in Pennsylvania. In addition to selling books, the print shop sold stationery, soap, ointments, coffee, tea, fish, and cheese. All the while, Deborah supported his endeavors, acting as bookkeeper and raising all three of the children.

Ever pursuant of new adventures, Franklin decided to begin publishing his very own almanac. These books were extremely popular and profitable at the time. Nearly every colonial household owned an almanac, which had to be purchased anew each year. They included calendars, weather forecasts, tide charts, wisdom, agricultural advice, personal advice, and witty proverbs. Franklin's own version was called *Poor Richard's Almanack*. It was first published in 1733 and went on to sell thousands of copies year after year, helping to make him a very wealthy man.

In addition to his publishing ventures, Franklin also worked alongside his Junto comrades to bring new social services to the residents of Philadelphia. Working together, they established America's first lending library, called the Library Company of Philadelphia, which was incorporated in 1731. To this day, it remains free and open to the public. The Junto also founded the city's first firefighting company, as well as the city's first hospital and the first college, which would eventually become the University of Pennsylvania. They also founded the American Philosophical Society for Promoting Useful Knowledge, which allowed men living in the colonies to exchange ideas through the mail.

All the while, Franklin's printing business continued to flourish. As the colony's first official printer, he printed the paper money, laws, and other necessary items for public life. He began sponsoring print shops outside of Philadelphia, furnishing the supplies in return for a share of the profits. At one time, he had a hand in more than twenty-four shops located from the tip of New England to the Caribbean islands.

By the age of forty-two, Franklin had made enough money to comfortably retire. He left the shop to his foreman, David Hall, though Franklin would be paid half of the firm's profits for the next eighteen years. Though he stepped down from his

The Library Company of Philadelphia still stands where it was built, and it continues to be free and open to the public. It offers a large collection of rare books, photographs, works of art, and more.

business, he would always identify proudly as a printer. In fact, Franklin's last will and testament, which was written in his eighty-third year, just before his death, started with the words, "I Benjamin Franklin of Philadelphia, Printer ... "[7]

Retirement?

Retirement for Benjamin Franklin wasn't marked by years of leisure time. In fact, the move away from his print business coincided with the most eventful decades of the man's life. His governmental career began in 1751, when Franklin assumed a seat in the Pennsylvania Assembly, the colony's ruling body, following the death of one of its members. Franklin had volunteered as a clerk of the assembly since 1736, but that was a tedious job that gave him little experience. Now, as a member of the twenty-six-man assembly, Franklin was able to dominate debates and cement his role as a civic leader for the colony. Franklin said of the role, "I conceived my becoming a member would enlarge my power of doing good. I would not however insinuate that my ambition was not flattered by all these promotions. It certainly was. For considering my low beginning they were great things to me."[8] At this time, he also installed his son, William, as the new clerk.

It was in these early years of retirement that Franklin found more time to actively pursue scientific experiments. While he had always been a curious child, creating his own inventions from a young age, Franklin was able to truly focus on science and innovation in his retired years. Some were practical, while others were pure fantasy. He worked with a friend from the Junto to run experiments on colors and sunlight absorption, placing cloth patches of various colors in a bed of snow. Then they measured the amount of snowmelt under each patch in an attempt to gauge how much the sun heated the different colors. They noted that dark colors absorb heat better than light colors. He also ran experiments on indoor heating. Franklin had noticed that when conventional fireplaces were used in homes (as most were in the 1700s), much of the hot air went out the chimney, while all that was left inside the home was smoke. So he invented a hooded iron stove, now called the Franklin stove, that burned less wood and produced more heat. Warm air went into the room while smoke was directed up the chimney. Though this was an extremely useful invention, Franklin refused to patent it, asserting confidently, "As we enjoy great advantages from the inventions of others, we should

FRANKLIN'S FIRST INVENTION

Benjamin Franklin didn't wait until retirement to start inventing. In fact, his first creation was introduced when he was only eleven years old! Living in Boston, Franklin always admired the water and wanted to learn to swim. He read *The Art of Swimming* in order to teach himself the basics, but then he wanted to go faster. So he fashioned for himself a pair of wooden planks, oval shaped, with holes through their middles. When the planks were grasped with one's hands, they gave extra thrust in the water, acting like "fins." He also fashioned a pair of boards that were strapped to his feet. It worked—Franklin was able to swim faster, though he later noted that the fins made his wrists tired and the boards made swimming a rather awkward endeavor.

be glad of an opportunity to serve others by an invention of ours, and this we should do freely and generously."[9] Of course, Franklin had already made his fortune. He was not in want of money. It was in this time period, too, that Franklin would conduct his famous kite-and-key experiment that would bring

Franklin's face has appeared on official documents and currencies throughout US history, including this five-cent postage stamp, originally released in 1847.

new insight into the ways in which scientists and laypeople thought about electricity.

Franklin's years of experimentation were well mixed with his time in public service. Around 1753, he was put in charge of the colonial postal service. This job was an appointment made by the king of England, and it gave Franklin the title of co-deputy postmaster. In this role, Franklin helped to strengthen the colonies' sense of unity and common desires. In 1775, he would become the first postmaster general of the United States. However, in the 1750s, the United States didn't exist yet. It would take many more years of struggle before the country gained independence, and Franklin would be heavily involved in that process.

Building to Independence

In 1757, Franklin would once again return to London. He was sent by the Pennsylvania Assembly in order to protest against the proprietors of the colony, the William Penn family, and their authority to King George II. His goal was to persuade the king to force the Penn family to pay taxes and to end their right to overrule the Pennsylvania legislature. While there, he became a leading spokesman for the interests of the colonists. Georgia, New Jersey, and Massachusetts all appointed him as their direct agent to the Crown. He stayed in London and Europe for eighteen years, traveling around but always using London as his home base. Sadly, while he was in Europe, Franklin's devoted wife, Deborah, passed away. After years of writing to Franklin and struggling to live a lonely life back in the colonies, Deborah died of stroke on December 14, 1774.

It was during these years that sentiments toward an American revolution were heating up back home. In 1775, as Franklin traveled back to Pennsylvania on a ship, the Revolutionary War broke out. There had been a huge change in public opinion about the possibility of independence. Though he was approaching old age, Franklin dug in and set to work helping to create a brand new nation.

In June 1776, he joined the Committee of Five, which drafted the Declaration of Independence. Thomas Jefferson largely wrote the declaration, but Franklin made several key changes, and his name is one of the signatures to appear on the document.

From 1776 to 1785, Franklin worked as the ambassador to France. While in France, he not only continued his scientific experiments, inventing bifocals among other things, but he also deepened his relationship with the French in order to secure their help with the Revolutionary War. Eventually, France sent thousands of soldiers to the colonies, helping them to gain independence in 1783 after many years of fighting.

Once home in Pennsylvania in 1785, Benjamin Franklin was treated as an honored champion of American independence. His portrait was painted, and would later hang in the National Portrait Gallery. He served as a delegate to the Philadelphia Convention and would be the only Founding Father to sign all four of the major founding documents: the Declaration of Independence, the Treaty of Alliance with France, the Treaty of Paris (which ended the war), and the US Constitution.

In his final years of life, Franklin stayed busier than ever. He donated to the opening of Franklin & Marshall College (which bears his name even today), finished his autobiography, and became president of the Pennsylvania Abolition Society. He also finally freed his slaves after a lifetime of slaveholding, including two slaves, Peter and King, who he had kept with him at all times while abroad.

As Franklin aged, his struggles with obesity resulted in health problems, including gout. The signing of the US Constitution in 1787 was one of the last times Franklin was seen in public. On April 17, 1790, he died from a pleuritic attack at his home in Philadelphia. He was eighty-four years old. He is interred at Christ Church Burial Ground in Philadelphia. Although around 1728, as a young man, Franklin had composed what he hoped to be his own epitaph, his grave simply reads "Benjamin and Deborah Franklin." While the more elaborate epitaph never came to fruition on his grave, it survives in print:

> The Body of
> B. Franklin,
> Printer;
> Like the Cover of an old Book,
> Its Contents torn out,
> And stript of its Lettering and Gilding,
> Lies here, Food for Worms.
> But the Work shall not be wholly lost:
> For it will, as he believ'd, appear once more,
> In a new & more perfect Edition,
> Corrected and amended
> By the Author.
> He was born Jan. 6. 1706.
> Died 17— [10]

CHAPTER THREE

Key Relationships

It is a fairly uncomplicated task to describe many of Benjamin Franklin's relationships through his long and busy life. He kept very few enemies and even fewer friends. His relationship with his brother James soured and became rather abusive following the Silence Dogood letters. His marriage to Deborah Read was loving and supportive, but also marred by Franklin's lack of fidelity. He remained close to his daughter, Sarah, throughout his entire life, and forever mourned the loss of his son, Francis. He also developed close friendships with many of his contemporaries, including the Founding Fathers.

The "Committee of Five" who were tasked with drafting the Declaration of Independence included John Adams (*far left*), Benjamin Franklin (*far right*), and Thomas Jefferson (*second from right*).

Thomas Jefferson

Thomas Jefferson, who wrote the Declaration of Independence, did not get along swimmingly with all of the Founding Fathers. He kept up a bitter rivalry with John Adams for many years, until their late-in-life reconciliation, and political differences with George Washington drove him far apart from the president. Jefferson even refused to attend Washington's funeral! However, Jefferson and Franklin maintained a sunny relationship throughout their lives. A few days after Franklin's death, Jefferson wrote to mutual friend Ferdinand Grand about Franklin, "The good old Doctor Franklin, so long an ornament of our country and I may say of the world, has at length closed his eminent career."[1] Jefferson knew that Franklin was not only a worldwide celebrity, but he was his own close friend. Their friendship began in 1775, at the Second Continental Congress. Benjamin Franklin was there to represent Pennsylvania, while Thomas

While Franklin (*left*) didn't have a perfect relationship with everyone he worked with, he did maintain a friendship with Thomas Jefferson (*right*) throughout his life.

Jefferson was representing Virginia. Both men supported resistance against Great Britain, though not all members of the Congress held that same view. Due to their common feelings, the two men became fast friends.

When it came time to draft the Declaration of Independence, Jefferson was chosen as the principal author, but Franklin was set apart as one of just four other men who provided assistance. They worked closely together on the document. Later, he and Franklin spent many months together in Paris, France, where Franklin served as the ambassador and Jefferson negotiated commercial treaties with France and several other European countries. He taught Jefferson many of the secrets to successful diplomacy, taking him under his professional wing. When Jefferson succeeded Franklin as American ambassador to France in 1785, the French foreign minister asked, "It is you who replace Dr. Franklin?" Jefferson replied, "No one can replace him, Sir; I am only his successor."[2] The two kept up a written correspondence over the years. Jefferson would often sign his letters to Franklin, "Your Excellency's most obedient & most humble Servt."[3]

George Washington

While Benjamin Franklin counted Thomas Jefferson as a close friend, President George Washington was more of a professional acquaintance, albeit one who he communicated with often and with whom he rarely disagreed. Franklin was quite a bit older than the president, having been born about twenty-six years earlier. Their paths crossed frequently, and the two began exchanging letters about important political business as early as 1756, twenty years before the American Revolution. In Franklin's last months of life, the two exchanged friendly, warm correspondence. In his last letter to Franklin, just months before his death, the then president wrote:

> If to be venerated for benevolence—if to be admired for talent—if to be esteemed for patriotism—if to be beloved for philanthropy can gratify the human mind, you must have the pleasing consolation to know that you have not lived in vain; and I flatter my self that it will not be ranked among the least grateful occurrences of your life to be assured that so long as I retain my memory—you will be thought on with respect, veneration and affection by Dear Sir Your sincere friend and obedient Hble Servant[4]

The two men always kept up mutual respect and admiration. In Franklin's will, he demonstrated his great affection for his friend and fellow revolutionary, bequeathing Washington the gold-capped walking stick that Franklin had accepted in 1783 as America's diplomat in France.

Other Founding Fathers

When it comes to the other Founding Fathers, such as James Monroe, Alexander Hamilton, and James Madison, Benjamin Franklin may not be remembered as their good friend or enemy, but rather as a contemporary, one who worked closely with them but held no special, particular relationship. John Adams may be the slight exception. In one letter to Benjamin Rush, Adams wrote of his worst nightmare, "The history of our Revolution will be one continued lie from one end to the other. The essence of the whole will be that Dr. Franklin's electric rod smote the earth and out sprang George Washington."[5] This was written in 1790, the year of Franklin's death, and says more about Adams's concerns about his own relative celebrity and concerns about the telling of history than it does about his personal relationship with Franklin.

Franklin's Junto

While Benjamin Franklin certainly had positive working relationships with the other Founding Fathers toward the end of his career and life, in his younger years he purposefully built relationships through the creation and continuation of his own social club. Founded in Philadelphia in the fall of 1727, Franklin and twelve of his friends formed the Junto Club, also known as the Leather Apron Club because tradesmen like Franklin often wore leather aprons to work. The other members were tradesmen and artisans, all white males, who met each Friday evening to discuss issues that they deemed important, such as morality, politics, and philosophy. The club lasted over thirty-eight years. It often worked together to make improvements to their city, including adding a city watch, a fire company, a library, a hospital, and other public projects. Among the original members were Thomas Godfrey (mathematician and glass worker), Joseph Breintall (writer), Steven Potts (Keimer's employee), William Maugridge (mechanic and cabinetmaker), William Parsons (shoemaker), Hugh Meredith (Keimer's employee and business partner of Franklin), Robert Grace (wealthy gentleman), George Webb (Keimer's apprentice), William Coleman (merchant), Nicholas Scull (surveyor), and John Jones (shoemaker). Franklin thought of these eleven men as more than just his friends. Together, they were thought workers, going about the business of expanding their minds and their city.

Franklin wrote a set of questions to guide discussion at meetings. They included the following, a partial listing, though there were twenty-four questions in all:

Have you met with anything in the author you last read, remarkable, or suitable to be communicated to the Junto? Particularly in history, morality, poetry, physics, travels, mechanic arts, or other parts of knowledge?

What new story have you lately heard agreeable for telling in conversation?

Has any citizen in your knowledge failed in his business lately, and what have you heard of the cause?

Have you lately heard of any citizen's thriving well, and by what means?

Have you lately heard how any present rich man, here or elsewhere, got his estate?

Do you know of any fellow citizen, who has lately done a worthy action, deserving praise and imitation? or who has committed an error proper for us to be warned against and avoid?

What unhappy effects of intemperance have you lately observed or heard? of imprudence? of passion? or of any other vice or folly?

What happy effects of temperance? of prudence? of moderation? or of any other virtue?

Have you or any of your acquaintances been lately sick or wounded? If so, what remedies were used, and what were their effects?

Who do you know that are shortly going [on] voyages or journeys, if one should have occasion to send by them?[6]

These questions served as a guide to the Junto meetings, setting off discussions that would then twist and turn through new ideas, relationships, problems, and questions. Philosophical issues were worked through, and new business ideas were formed. Many of the actions that the group took, such as forming the first library and volunteer fire station, came about through discussions just like these. When they asked a question such as, "What does it mean to thrive?" The answers that resulted were not just thoughts to muse upon, but calls to action that eventually ended in community-supported change.

Franklin's Protégé: Thomas Paine

Benjamin Franklin and Thomas Paine first met in London between 1772 and 1773, while Franklin was representing the colonies in the run-up to the American Revolution. Franklin, as usual, was surrounding himself with friends and contemporaries who were interested in the American cause, and Thomas Paine was one of those people. He was in London to advocate on behalf of tax collectors in Lewes, England. He was hoping for higher wages and better working conditions. While he was in London, he practiced his debating skills by delivering passionate speeches on behalf of the common people.

Franklin took note of Paine's talents and urged him to sail for Philadelphia, which Paine did in the fall of 1774, bringing with him a letter of introduction that Franklin wrote for him to take to America. Franklin recommended his friend for

Is Thomas Paine, shown in this portrait, the sole author of *Common Sense*, or did Benjamin Franklin play a major role in the writing of the document? We may never know for sure.

work as a clerk or a surveyor. Franklin would return a year later, in 1775.

In that same year, Paine wrote a passionate pamphlet. He showed it to Franklin for comment, and some historians assert that Franklin made many comments during the initial writing. It is hard to know for sure just how much influence Franklin had on the original document. We do know that the document made a splash in American bookstores when published in 1776 as *Common Sense*. Since the pamphlet was first published anonymously, many readers suspected that Benjamin Franklin was the author! The pamphlet helped to bolster colonists against the Crown and toward independence.

In the years following, Paine and Franklin would maintain a rigorous correspondence through letters on subjects both professional and personal. Franklin helped Paine with many of his letters and essays, even those such as *Age of Reason*, which infuriated many of the other Founding Fathers, including John Adams and Benjamin Rush. Paine would manage to stay involved in French and American politics, eventually diving headfirst into the French Revolution and dying with very little money to his name.

Franklin's Relationships with Women

While it may seem as though Benjamin Franklin enjoyed a life that was entirely made up of the business and whims of other men while his wife waited patiently at home, he actually kept up a very social life with women that he met throughout his travels, and enjoyed a relationship all the while with Deborah, who raised his children and supported him from near and far.

For his time, Franklin enjoyed what we might think of today as "celebrity" status. He was a well-known diplomat,

FRANKLIN'S RELATIONSHIP TO RELIGION AND GOD

Benjamin Franklin, writing in his own autobiography, was a self-proclaimed deist. Though he believed in God and was raised as a Puritan, he had a kind of Christianity that was focused more on how one lives than what one believes. At times, he did consider some radical anti-Christian beliefs and doubted some tenants of Protestant faith, but he ultimately settled on the idea that Christianity fostered virtue and was therefore good. In fact, during the Constitutional Convention in 1787, Franklin even proposed that the convention open its sessions with prayer. Though the others at the convention would vote down this proposal, Franklin's doctrineless, moralizing form of Christianity would become somewhat of a model for the popular forms of spirituality we see burgeoning across the United States today.

thinker, wealthy businessman, and scientist. Throughout this life, Franklin described himself as fit and attractive, and it seems he had no shortage of adoring women who called after him. Deborah, his long-time common-law wife, seems to have tolerated her husband's behavior toward these women, though there was little she had the right (and time) to do. While her husband was building his print shop business, she was working in the background as his bookkeeper, all the while raising his children, including the one he produced out of wedlock, and keeping their Philadelphia home in running order. Historians suggest that most of Franklin's dalliances were fairly innocent, not more than flirtatious relationships mostly conducted through letters. In French, these relationships were referred to as *amitie amoureuse*, or "amorous friendship."

Franklin and Deborah's relationship was not particularly passionate, though they became engaged at a young age, right when Franklin moved to Philadelphia in 1723. For eighteen of the forty-four years of their union, however, the two lived apart. Deborah never joined Franklin for any of his overseas trips, even those that lasted many years. Back home, she acted as postmistress and oversaw the building of a larger house for the family. At one time, Stamp Act rioters threatened their home, and Deborah and her brother were forced to fend them off. As the years apart ticked by, their estrangement grew, until Deborah passed in 1774, alone.

Some of Franklin's suitors have been noted in his letters, such as Catharine Ray, who he met in the winter of 1754 while inspecting New England's postal network. He was forty-eight years old and she was twenty-three. After a few days of travel together to Rhode Island in a winter storm, they exchanged flirtatious letters, but never met again. Ray eventually married William Greene Jr., the future governor of Rhode Island.

When he was in his seventies, Franklin met Anne Louise d'Hardancourt Brillon de Jouy, who played beautiful music on the harpsichord and piano. She invited him to tea, parties, and chess games. They developed a relationship, though she referred to him as "Cher Papa," a name that caught on widely while Franklin lived in France. Though he protested, their father-daughter relationship remained. Around the same time, Franklin met Anne-Catherine de Ligniville d'Autricourt, a descendant of Austrian nobility, and better known as Madame Helvétius. She held court over a salon of Enlightenment-era philosophers, which Franklin regarded as an intellectual getaway. He proposed marriage to her. She rebuked him, however, and he finally decided to return home to America.

Historians have also guessed that Franklin carried on a long relationship with Margaret Stevenson, who owned a four-story townhouse in London where Franklin lived for fifteen years. He also engaged in a very long and friendly correspondence with Margaret's young daughter, Polly. For a time, he wished that Polly would marry his son William, but William was in love with another woman. Decades later, after the deaths of Deborah and Polly's own husband, Polly and her three children traveled to Philadelphia to live near Franklin until his death.

Son and Enemy

Most of the relationships that Benjamin Franklin formed throughout his accomplished life were positive ones built on trust, mutual agreement, and even flirtation. However, his relationship with his son William was one that disappointed him greatly and hurt him to his core. As Franklin described it, "Nothing," he said toward the end of the war, "has ever hurt

Benjamin Franklin's son William wore his best clothing for this formal portrait. His loyalty to Great Britain eventually destroyed his relationship with his father.

me so much … as to find myself deserted in my old age by my only son."[7] Franklin's other son, Francis, had died at age four of smallpox. William Franklin's crime? He was a Loyalist, just like about 20 percent of the white American population in the colonies during the war.

Franklin had raised William from a young age to be a loyal servant, and that is how he remained into adulthood, even while Franklin's thoughts on the subject evolved over time. While his father chose to reject the Crown and fight for independence, William chose to stay loyal. During the war, he was imprisoned, his property was confiscated, and his wife died. William insisted that she died of a broken heart while he was imprisoned, and as his was similarly broken, he wanted nothing more than to reconcile with his father at war's end. But Franklin wouldn't have it. He left his son nearly nothing in his will, writing, "The part he acted against me in the late War," Franklin bitterly explained, "which is of public Notoriety, will account for my leaving him no more of an Estate he endeavored to deprive me of."[8] William sailed to England in 1782 for exile and never saw his father again.

CHAPTER FOUR

Franklin's Creations

Benjamin Franklin's contributions to the revolution and the building of a new nation cannot be understated. He is remembered as a Founding Father, a signer of many of America's most important documents, and one of many who helped form the United States in its earliest inception. However, Franklin also spent much of his life as a scientist and inventor, and in those realms his contributions were many, varied, and significant. Without Franklin's work, our lives would carry on without several significant inventions and scientific discoveries. Fortunately, today we get to enjoy the fruits of his intellectual labor.

Franklin conducted many experiments throughout his lifetime, but his most memorable trial was probably the famous kite-and-key experiment.

The Inventor

Throughout his long life, Franklin continuously looked for practical ways in which he could improve his life and the lives of others. He observed, thought, read, and experimented. Most of his experiments and inventions occurred after he retired from printing at the age of forty-two. The following is an incomplete listing of Franklin's most famous and most significant discoveries and inventions.

Lightning Rod

When many people, children and adults alike, think of Benjamin Franklin, they often name him as one of the inventors of electricity, or at least believe that he played a large role in electricity's discovery. This is not entirely true. The basics of electric current were discovered by others, many of whom, such as William Gilbert and Stephen Gray, were studied by Franklin in his quest to learn more about electric power. Where Franklin did make strides was in our understanding of electric current and charge.

His journey began in the summer of 1743, when Franklin watched a common showman do a trick. Silk cords dangled from the ceiling of a tent. A man tied the cords around a boy's ankles and wrists so that the boy was strung up in midair. Then, he carefully rubbed the boy's bare feet with a glass tube. He touched the boy's forehead, and golden sparks flickered out, just like magic! Franklin was quite taken with the circus act and wanted to figure out what was behind this "sparking power." He decided to investigate.

In order to dive deeper, Franklin borrowed a friction machine from a friend. These machines were the very first electrostatic generators. They involved a rotating wheel that turned a glass sphere. A person would place his or her hands or a wool cloth on the rotating glass sphere, which would, in turn, produce static electricity. When Franklin used the machine, he noticed that the sparks flying from it looked curiously like lightning bolts. He continued to read about electricity, learning that metal attracts power and that some materials won't carry power at all. He hypothesized that lightning might carry electricity, and he decided to test it out. What happened next would define popular stories about Benjamin Franklin for the rest of his life, and in the decades following his death.

According to legend, Franklin took his son William out into a field on a stormy day in June 1752. He carried a kite. On the top he had attached a metal wire. To Franklin's mind, if lightning was electricity, the metal would attract lightning. He tied a long string from the center of the kite and an iron key to the bottom of the string. At the end of the string he attached a silk ribbon, because electric power does not run through silk. This was a safety measure.

In the field, there were dark clouds overhead. William launched the kite into the sky on a wave of wind. He held onto the silk string and watched the kite jerk around, while Franklin stood in an old shed nearby. All of a sudden, the string's fibers began to stand on end. Franklin remembered the friction machine and the ways in which it made his brown hair stand on end—it must be electricity! When Franklin touched the key with his knuckle, a spark shocked him before he even reached the key. The electricity had moved from the sky to the metal at the top of the kite, and then down through the string and into the key.

No, Benjamin Franklin did not invent electricity. But his groundbreaking experiment led him and other people to ask many new questions about the ways in which electricity works. He kept experimenting. Some others tried to redo his experiment, getting mixed results. A few of these people were so physically shocked by the electricity from lightning that they died.

One invention that did come out of the experiment was the lightning rod. In the eighteenth century, lightning often destroyed city buildings made primarily of wood. Churches were especially susceptible, since they were so tall—often the tallest structures in town. Based on his experiment with the key, Franklin decided to affix a metal rod to the top of such buildings, and wire them to the ground with a cable, extracting the electricity from the cloud and putting it safely in the ground before it hurt the building. His idea caught on quickly, first on countryside churches that needed protection as the tallest buildings in the area, and then across the world, in all sorts of tall buildings. It certainly saved both buildings and people from harm, and the science behind lightning rods is still put to use in tall buildings to this day.

In the midst of these electrical experiments, Franklin also came up with many of the terms that we use today, including battery, charge, conductor, plus, minus, positively, negatively, and condenser. In a letter to Peter Collinson, a friend and patron of the Junto, Franklin attempted to describe his findings: "Fire only circulates. Hence have arisen some new items among us. We say B (and other Bodies alike circumstanced) are electricised *positively*; A *negatively*; Or rather B is electricised *plus* and A *minus* … *These terms* we may use till philosophers give us better."[1] The words often eluded him, especially because the science was so new, but in letters like these, Franklin worked out the terms that we would one day come to use in casual conversation.

In another letter, Franklin wrote, "I feel a Want of Terms here and doubt much whether I shall be able to make this intelligible."[2] He must have eventually become somewhat comfortable, of course, because his findings and words have survived over many centuries.

Bifocals

As many people approach old age, they often find themselves in need of bifocals, which are glasses with two types of lenses—one for seeing objects up close, and another for seeing objects far away. The lenses are usually divided between top and bottom. This is why you may see an older person moving their head up and down, finding the correct angle at which to view a book or a faraway sign. This technology was invented by Franklin, who noticed his own eyesight growing worse as he grew older. His vision became blurry when he read things up close and when he looked into the distance. For a time, Franklin owned two pairs of eyeglasses and switched between them whenever necessary, but this became quite a bother. In order to make his life easier, he invented what he called "double spectacles." He took the lenses from his two pairs of glasses, cut them in half horizontally, and refashioned them into a single pair of glasses. The lenses for distance were on the top and reading lenses were on the bottom. In an August 1784 letter to his friend George Whatley, Franklin wrote:

> I cannot distinguish a letter even of large print; but am happy in the invention of double spectacles, which serving for distant objects as well as near ones, make my eyes as useful to me as ever they were: If all the other defects and infirmities were as easily and cheaply remedied, it would be worth while for friends to live a good deal longer.[3]

THE LIBRARY COMPANY OF PHILADELPHIA (LCP)

One of Franklin's most beloved contributions to his city would be the Library Company of Philadelphia. This offshoot of the Junto at first was constructed in order to share books—which were expensive, few, and far between in colonial Pennsylvania—between members of the Junto and residents of the town. At first, the library was only open on Saturdays, for four hours in the afternoon, but it soon expanded its reach.

Currently, it houses a historically significant collection of books, manuscripts, maps, and pamphlets, many from the revolution era. It holds first editions of both Herman Melville's *Moby Dick* (1851) and Walt Whitman's *Leaves of Grass* (1855). The library remains free and open to the public, just as Franklin wished.

Unfortunately, none of Franklin's original glasses, bifocal or otherwise, have been found among his possessions, so we are unable to hold his original glasses in hand or look to them as an artifact.

Gulf Stream

The Atlantic Ocean has within it a powerful current. A current is a directed movement of water generated by wind, water density, and tides, among other things. This particular current is known as the Gulf Stream, and it begins in the Gulf of Mexico, flows into the Atlantic Ocean at Florida's southern tip, and then accelerates along the eastern coastline of the United States and Newfoundland, Canada. It was Benjamin Franklin who published the very first map of this important current in 1770. He had always held an interest in ocean currents, perhaps due in part to his upbringing near Boston Harbor and his dreams of becoming a sailor. Eventually, though, his interest grew as he became comfortable in his role as deputy postmaster of the colonies and desired to gain a better understanding of currents as they affected communication between the colonies and England. At that time, mail was transported via ships. Ocean currents would have an effect on how fast ships could move and in what directions they could go.

On a visit to England in 1768, Franklin learned that it took British mail several weeks longer to reach New York City than it took an American ship to reach Rhode Island. Franklin's cousin, Timothy Folger, was a Nantucket whaling captain with wisdom about the sea. He explained to Franklin that American merchant ships crossed the Gulf Stream, though he didn't have that name for it. Folger just knew that mail ships ran against the current, slowing them down, and American ships traveled with it. The merchant ships were able to track whale behavior,

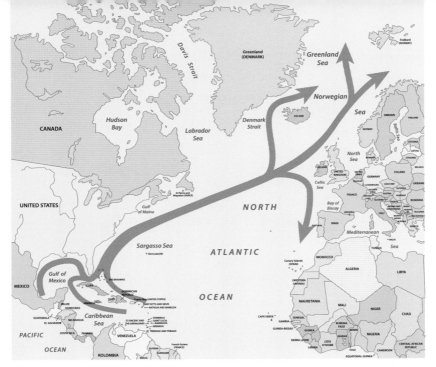

Franklin helped identify and popularize the idea of the Gulf Stream, a current that runs northeast from the Gulf of Mexico.

water temperature, and changes in the water's color in order to put themselves on the faster path. Franklin became enamored with this science, working directly with ship captains to chart what he would call the Gulf Stream. He published the chart in England in 1770, France in 1778, and the United States in 1786. Eventually, knowledge of the Gulf Stream would help the British cut their sailing time to the United States down by a full two weeks. During the American Revolution, Franklin gave Gulf Stream maps to America's French allies. Though Franklin remains indebted to the experienced sailors, including his cousin, who helped him understand the Gulf Stream, his decision to map it, as well as his general celebrity, has made him the "inventor" of the Gulf Stream map.

Glass Armonica

Sometimes, Franklin found inspiration for his inventions in the most common of places. When attending dinner parties, Franklin noticed the way dinner guests would occasionally "play" their wineglasses by rubbing the rim of it to produce a musical tone. During his European travels, he even attended an amateur concert in which a person performed on a set of "singing" glasses. Franklin was intrigued. In 1761, he came up with his own instrument based on the science. He worked with a glassblower in London to make a few dozen glass bowls of varying sizes. They were fitted one into the next with cork. The bowls were carefully sized to produce specific tones and painted in different colors so as to mark them as different notes. A hole was bored into the center of each bowl and an iron rod ran the length of them. At the end, the rod was attached to a wheel that the player turned using a pedal. The player would moisten his or her fingers and touch them to the edges of the spinning bowls, creating music. This instrument became known as the glass armonica (or harmonica).

The glass armonica sat in a handsome wooden case, appearing almost like a small desk. Over the course of the eighteenth century, it would become a celebrated instrument. Franklin played it for audiences himself, carefully eking out Scottish songs and original compositions. In time, Beethoven, Mozart, and other composers would write music for the instrument. Of course, as with his other inventions, Franklin refused to patent the armonica, even though over five thousand had been built by the time of his death.

Oddly, over time, the glass armonica came to be associated with sickness and death. Players complained of symptoms such as muscle spasms, nervousness, cramps, and dizziness, which may have been caused by the lead from the bowls and paint.

This invention of Franklin's is known as a bowl organ or hydrocrystalophone. One of Franklin's original glass armonicas, it can be found at the Franklin Institute in Philadelphia.

In one incident, a child died while in the audience of a glass armonica performance, and the instrument was subsequently banned in a few towns. Some were disturbed by the tones themselves. However, Franklin continued to play the instrument until his death, with no mention of symptoms. The instrument was at its height of popularity while he was alive, but by the 1820s it was nearly forgotten.

Other Inventions

Franklin had so many discoveries and inventions that some have been lost to popular memory. Not all have stood the test of time. Over the years, Franklin invented the following:

- A divided soup bowl, with one main compartment surrounded by "mini bowls," for use when eating soup on ships. When the ship tipped, soup would flow into the mini bowls instead of out onto the floor.

- A chair with a set of short steps on a hinge, so that it could serve as both a place to rest and a stepladder in a library.
- One of the very first odometers, used to help Franklin chart distances between America's major postal centers. It wasn't the first—the odometer was invented in ancient Roman times. However, Franklin put his own odometer to new and practical use.
- A drawing that has come to be known as America's first political cartoon. While working at the *Pennsylvania Gazette*, his newspaper, Franklin published a drawing of a snake cut into eight pieces that represented the colonies. In 1752, when the cartoon was published, the colonies were at the brink of war with France. Franklin's cartoon, which said "Join, Or Die," suggested that the colonies needed to be unified in order to protect against attack. Later, though the cartoon was created during the French and Indian War, it would become a popular symbol of the American Revolution.
- A "long arm" tool for reaching books on high library shelves. The arm consisted of a piece of wood with two "fingers" on the end. When he pulled a cable, the fingers would grip a book. Though this type of device isn't usually seen in libraries today, the technology remains in "litter grabbers" that are used in parks and public spaces, as well as special devices for shorter people and the elderly, who often need a bit of help picking up objects that are just out of reach.

Autobiography

In addition to his scientific inventions, Franklin created many bodies of written work, including essays, countless letters, and, eventually, his very own autobiography. The traditional name for this book about Franklin's life is *The Autobiography of Benjamin Franklin*, though throughout his life, the author referred to the work as his memoirs. The book has become a well-known and influential example of the autobiography form.

The book was first published in 1791, after Franklin's death. It is divided into four parts. The first, addressed to his son William, details his life up until his marriage and the beginning of the Junto. Part Two discusses his plans for the Library Company of Philadelphia and lays out his list of thirteen moral virtues. Part Three dives into his experiments, religion, the death of his son Francis, the French and Indian War, and other events throughout his life. The final part is brief, written between the fall of 1789 and Franklin's death. It details some of what occurred on Franklin's trip to London on behalf of the colonies. Most critics consider Franklin's autobiography to be down-to-Earth, approachable, and altogether the makings of an American classic.

One of the most memorable aspects of Franklin's autobiography may be his "thirteen virtues," a list, compiled when Franklin was only twenty years old, of virtues that would help Franklin develop his own character. He considered them necessary or desirable for all people, not just himself. They are as follows:

- **Temperance**. Eat not to dullness; drink not to elevation.
- **Silence**. Speak not but what may benefit others or yourself; avoid trifling conversation.
- **Order**. Let all your things have their places; let each part of your business have its time.
- **Resolution**. Resolve to perform what you ought; perform without fail what you resolve.

- **Frugality**. Make no expense but to do good to others or yourself; i.e., waste nothing.
- **Industry**. Lose no time; be always employ'd in something useful; cut off all unnecessary actions.
- **Sincerity**. Use no hurtful deceit; think innocently and justly, and, if you speak, speak accordingly.
- **Justice**. Wrong none by doing injuries, or omitting the benefits that are your duty.
- **Moderation**. Avoid extremes; forbear resenting injuries so much as you think they deserve.
- **Cleanliness**. Tolerate no uncleanliness in body, cloaths, or habitation.
- **Tranquillity**. Be not disturbed at trifles, or at accidents common or unavoidable.
- **Chastity**. Rarely use venery but for health or offspring, never to dullness, weakness, or the injury of your own or another's peace or reputation.
- **Humility**. Imitate Jesus and Socrates.[4]

In order to acquire these virtues, Franklin advised, "I judg'd it would be well not to distract my attention by attempting the whole at once, but to fix it on one of them at a time."[5] Franklin hoped to succeed at one virtue completely before moving on to the next. Of course, some of these were lofty goals. But once Franklin thought he had mastered cleanliness, he would move on to attempting to be more tranquil, and so on. Unfortunately, Franklin never recorded in writing whether he had accomplished all of these virtues. They would later be mocked by some other writers, including Mark Twain, who found the virtues to be of very little use.

CHAPTER FIVE

Interpretation and Influence

Benjamin Franklin is one of the earliest celebrities the United States has known. Throughout his life and in the centuries following his death, he has been admired. Some might argue that he is one of the most admired and revered Founding Fathers, if not *the* most popular. As a well-known figure, his likeness appears on television, in cartoons, on various products, and remains memorialized on American money and statues, among many other things. However, Franklin hasn't always been so beloved. Some critics have called out his writing, his womanizing, his opportunism, and even his potential heresy. If nothing else, it remains clear that people hold a diverse array of opinions on Benjamin Franklin, and there are few people who have escaped his influence over time.

Depictions of Franklin in adulthood almost always include his glasses, long hair, and a serious facial expression.

Who Was Benjamin Franklin?

One of the most elusive parts of the public's understanding of Benjamin Franklin is who, exactly, he was. Did he belong to a certain discipline over others? If so, which one? He was a literary author, but he was also heavily involved in both politics and science. He helped shape the course of the nation, all the while coming up with new inventions, making his fortune as a printer, traveling the world, and acting as a diplomat. Though Franklin was all of these things at once, the multiplicity of his interests does make it difficult to see Franklin as one whole person, rather than a character made up of several different individuals. When he is critiqued and written about, descriptions of Franklin run the gamut—at various times he is understood to be a practical businessman, a wizened grandfather of the nation, a poor-boy-turned-rich-man, a quirky scientist, and a romantic social butterfly. Paul Leicester Ford's 1899 biography is called *The Many-Sided Franklin*,[1] and the text is aptly named. Ford details Franklin's life as a printer, publisher, writer, journalist, politician, diplomat, scientist, humorist, and more.

Stepping through Franklin's life is not an easy journey. Though he is now deeply embedded into our national consciousness, no two individuals probably picture the exact same man when they think of Benjamin Franklin. In this way, he remains one of the most interesting characters in US history.

Franklin's Critics

Though Franklin can be considered an early American celebrity, he is not without his critics. After his autobiography was published, other authors and philosophers let their opinions be known. Their thoughts were varied, with many taking swipes at the Founding Father after his death, while others sought to remind the public of his virtues.

Mark Twain

On January 17, 1856, a young Samuel Clemens gave one of his very first comedic toasts—or "roasts," as they were more accurately described. Clemens, who would later be known

Mark Twain authored countless pieces of writing using several different pen names. Two of his most famous works are *The Adventures of Tom Sawyer* and *Adventures of Huckleberry Finn*.

as Mark Twain, would eventually become famous for these toasts. The first one was given during a celebration of the sesquicentennial of Benjamin Franklin's birth in which local printers got together and drank to one of the late, great men of their trade. Years later, Twain would be invited to speak again, and again on the occasion of Franklin's birth.

Though he was born in 1835, decades after Franklin's death, and never spent time with Franklin, Twain certainly held some strong opinions of him. In his own novels, he mocked Franklin. In *Pudd'nhead Wilson*, he opened each chapter with words from *Pudd'nhead Wilson's Calendar*, which was a clear parody of *Poor Richard's Almanack*. He felt that Franklin's maxims and public image were just that—an image that Franklin didn't truly live up to, not in his thirteen virtues or in any other way.

Twain was coming up during a time of greatly revived popularity for the late Benjamin Franklin. Biographies of the man were authored, dime novels about rags-to-riches boys became all the rage, and successful industrialists erected statues of Franklin. He was praised in print newspapers and magazines. But Twain took a completely different track.

In 1870, Mark Twain published "The Late Benjamin Franklin," a wordy complaint about Franklin's autobiography and the effect it had on fathers who used it as a child-rearing guide. He wrote:

> His maxims were full of animosity toward boys. Nowadays a boy cannot follow out a single natural instinct without tumbling over some of those everlasting aphorisms and hearing from Franklin, on the spot. If he buys two cents' worth of peanuts, his father says, "Remember what Franklin has said, my son—'A grout a day's a penny a year'"; and the

comfort is all gone out of those peanuts. If he wants to spin his top when he has done work, his father quotes, "Procrastination is the thief of time." If he does a virtuous action, he never gets anything for it, because "Virtue is its own reward."[2]

Twain complained about his own father's reading of Franklin and recommendations that Twain follow the virtues, quotes, and suggestions from Franklin's writings. He maintained that Franklin's words were "calculated to inflict suffering" upon young men and boys, because they set up standards that were impossible to follow, such as working in your parents' soap shop and then staying up all night to study algebra, while all the while being inherently virtuous and good.

In an 1869 letter that may have been Twain's inspiration for the piece, he wrote, "If it had not been for him, with his incendiary 'Early to bed and early to rise,' and all that sort of foolishness, I wouldn't have been so harried and worried and raked out of bed at such unseemly hours when I was young. The late Franklin was well enough in his way; but it would have looked more dignified in him to have gone on making candles and letting other people get up when they wanted to."[3] Twain seems to have held much derision toward Franklin, though one wonders if his feelings were mostly in jest, intended to spark lively discussion and laughs.

D. H. Lawrence

Another attack on Franklin's character and virtues came from D. H. Lawrence in his 1923 *Studies in Classic American Literature*. Lawrence directly questioned Franklin's ability, as well as the ability of any person, to change their life through a list of virtues willed into existence. He simply did not believe

D. H. Lawrence's huge body of work ranges from novels and short stories to travel books, poetry, translations, and even paintings.

that a person could perfect himself in the ways that Franklin suggested, writing, "I am not a mechanical contrivance."[4] In the text, he purports to both admire and dislike Franklin—he does not mince words. Then he has a little fun with Franklin's thirteen virtues, composing his own list.

Lawrence's heavy-handed takedown of Benjamin Franklin was both humorous and serious. In his thirteen "virtues" he aimed to directly contradict all of Franklin's own explanations, strongly opposing Franklin's ideas and the myth of perfection. He directly mocked Franklin's attempts at achieving moral perfection, which was not unlike Twain's own critique, but certainly had more fire behind it. His review was scathing, including lines like, "ORDER—Know that you are responsible to the gods inside you and to the men in whom the gods are manifest. Recognize your superiors and your inferiors, according to the gods. This is the root of all order," "SINCERITY—To be sincere is to remember that I am I, and that the other man is not me," "CLEANLINESS—Don't be too clean. It impoverishes the blood," and "HUMILITY—See all men and women according to the Holy Ghost that is within them. Never yield before the barren."[5]

US Constitution

While many writers would hold opinions about Benjamin Franklin's autobiography and even his personal character, most critics alive during his time were set up to battle with him over the work that was most important to the future of the country—the US Constitution.

In 1787, Franklin participated as a delegate to the Constitutional Convention in Philadelphia, over which George Washington presided. At this time, Franklin was

The Constitutional Convention was held at the old Pennsylvania State House, which is now known as Independence Hall. All told, the convention took about four months.

eighty-one years old and in generally poor health. He was the oldest delegate present, and actually had to be transported to the sessions in a sedan chair. He would die within the next few years, but not before he saw all of his work toward the revolution come to fruition.

In all, fifty-five delegates attended the Constitutional Convention sessions, with thirty-nine signing the document. These delegates had varying ideas about how the country should be organized and run, and it was their job to come to some sort of agreement, which was an incredibly difficult task. Franklin, for his part, believed that a committee should handle executive power, as it was too much to be placed on one person. Another Founding Father, Alexander Hamilton, strongly disagreed, desiring instead a single executive that would be appointed for life. The convention chose the middle ground, ruling that the country would have one executive, with balanced power and a limited term.

When it came to the legislature, Franklin desired a single legislative chamber. But most of the delegates pushed for equal representation of large and small states, which would likely necessitate a bicameral legislature, or one with two parts. It was Franklin who eventually helped the body come to a compromise, breaking the deadlock and creating the legislative system that we see today, with the lower house composed of representatives according to population and the upper house with an equal number from each state.

With these and other issues finally cleared up (how treaties should be signed, how roads should be built, etc.), the Constitution was finished in September 1787, though many delegates remained unhappy with the document. Franklin himself was not entirely pleased. As an ardent opponent of slavery, although he himself had slaves, he made a personal compromise and let the issue be ignored in the Constitutional Convention, though he had previously expressed that he was passionate about abolition. Unfortunately, Franklin's autobiographical account of his early life does not state his frank thoughts on the matter of the Constitution, except in the speech he gave at the end of the Convention. Franklin chose to make a passionate speech that helped to tip the votes in favor of signing the Constitution. His speech, which would be his final thoughts to the Constitutional Convention, were recorded by James Madison. In part, he said:

> I confess that I do not entirely approve of this Constitution at present, but Sir, I am not sure I shall never approve it: For having lived long, I have experienced many Instances of being oblig'd, by better Information or fuller Consideration, to change Opinions even on important Subjects, which I once thought right, but found to be otherwise. It is therefore that the older I grow the more apt I am to doubt my own Judgment, and to pay more Respect to the Judgment of others ... I doubt too whether any other Convention we can obtain, may be able to make a better Constitution: For when you assemble a Number of Men to have the Advantage of their joint Wisdom, you inevitably assemble with those Men all their Prejudices, their Passions, their Errors of Opinion, their local Interests, and their selfish Views. From such an Assembly can a perfect Production be expected? It therefore astonishes me, Sir, to find this System approaching so near to Perfection as it does; and I think it will astonish our Enemies, who are waiting with Confidence to hear

that our Councils are confounded ... and that our States are on the Point of Separation, only to meet hereafter for the Purpose of cutting one another's throats. Thus I consent, Sir, to this Constitution because I expect no better, and because I am not sure that it is not the best.[6]

To Franklin's chagrin, some of the delegates still refused to sign the document. In that stifling hot room in Philadelphia, Franklin worked to persuade most, but not all, delegates to sign. Edmund Randolph, George Mason, and Elbridge Gerry all refused to sign the document because it included no bill of rights in its original form. Franklin did succeed in convincing enough signers, though, and in helping to put together a Constitution that, while not perfect, was a solid starting point for the new nation. During his lifetime, Franklin would see ten constitutional amendments submitted for ratification, making up the Bill of Rights, though he would not live to see their completed ratification and inclusion in the Constitution.

Opponents in the Church

Perhaps one of the most surprising oppositions that Franklin ever faced was assertions from theologians that Franklin and his experiments were heretical in nature. For centuries, Protestant and Catholic churches had taught, based on specific biblical readings, that the air was filled with witches, demons, and devils. St. Augustine, St. Thomas Aquinas, Martin Luther, and others all asserted that the rain and winds were filled with spirits and devils. In Christian churches, lightning storms were warded off through prayer, holy water, and the consecration of church bells in the hopes that the bells might cast down

Today, many churches have lightning rods on top of their steeples in order to safely attract lightning bolts without fear of fire.

the spirits. Sadly, church towers were often hit by lightning, as they were the tallest structures in town, and bell ringers were occasionally electrocuted while ringing the bells.

In 1752, Franklin conducted his experiment with the iron key tied to the kite and flown about during a storm. While the question of lightning had long troubled the world's theologians, Franklin seemed to sum it all up with an easy answer: it was electricity, and it could be controlled with a simple lightning rod attached to the roof. Across Europe, mass displeasure fell

MONEY MAN

In addition to his work during the Revolutionary War years as a diplomat, writer, signer, thinker, and Founding Father, Benjamin Franklin also helped out in another huge way. He secured a large amount of money in order to fund the war.

While he was in France, Franklin didn't just convince the French government to provide the colonists with physical military support. Franklin, working with fellow diplomat Silas Deane, negotiated with France to provide the brand-new United States with six giant loans, nearly breaking the French Treasury. These loans were used to strengthen the American army, providing them with the necessary supplies and weapons to put up a real fight.

After the war, the United States nearly defaulted on its loans, leaving the finances with France unsettled until 1795, when American banker James Swan privately assumed the debt at a slightly higher interest rate. Thanks to Swan, Franklin's deal didn't turn out to be a bad one for the United States. In fact, without the loans, the patriots may not have been able to pay for the eight-year war.

on the lightning rod, as churchgoers thought of the tool as interfering with God's plans, be they destructive or otherwise. The Reverend Thomas Prince, pastor of Old South Church, even went so far as to blame the lightning rod, and Franklin, in 1755 for the Massachusetts earthquake that occurred that year. In his sermon, he suggested that Boston had more lightning rods than any other city in the area, and that Boston was affected terribly by the earthquake due to all of these sacrilegious items.

Though theologians were shaken up by this new invention's ability to control heaven's artillery, there was no ignoring the practicality of the rod. With them, the constant destruction of churches by lightning all but ceased completely. The theology was forced to bend to the science of the day. Franklin's invention would remain.

CHAPTER SIX

Remembering Benjamin Franklin

W hen people today think of Benjamin Franklin, any number of his roles and titles might come to mind. Some automatically place him within the context of the Founding Fathers, remembering the part he played in the writing of the Declaration of Independence and the US Constitution. Others consider him a scientist, perhaps misguidedly naming him as the "inventor of electricity," or recalling his experiment with the kite and key. A few may have read his autobiography and thus associate him with writing, printing, and travel, among other things. Franklin was incredibly multifaceted, which adds to his continuous popularity and celebrity in the world of early American characters. Woven throughout all of these roles was his earnest commitment to "American"

The centerpiece of the Benjamin Franklin National Memorial in Philadelphia is a statue of Franklin that weighs 30 tons (27 metric tons) and sits on a large marble pedestal.

values, his wisdom, diplomacy, and general capability that led him to successes on behalf of the young nation. Today, many Americans look to Franklin as a favorite Founding Father. He has left a lasting legacy on the country, and his celebrity "star" doesn't seem to be dimming any time soon.

Monuments and Memories

In the United States, Benjamin Franklin is remembered in a number of physical, honorary ways. His portrait hangs in the National Portrait Gallery, alongside presidents, first ladies, and other key figures. His face is also featured on the one hundred dollar bill, which is why they are commonly referred to as "Benjamins," "Franklins," or—simply—"Bens." It is one of only two bills that features a person other than a US president (the ten dollar bill, with Alexander Hamilton's portrait printed on it, is the other), and it has Independence Hall's image on the other side, unlike the other paper bills, on which there are images of buildings located in Washington, DC. Though in recent years, there has been a push to remove Andrew Jackson from the twenty dollar bill due to his slave ownership and the forcing of Cherokee people from their lands with the Indian Removal Act of 1830, there has been no such discussion of removing Franklin. Franklin was not a perfect man (he also owned slaves, and lived in colonial America, on land which had once belonged to Native Americans), but the general historical view of his character is positive.

Due to all of this positive energy surrounding Franklin's memory, Americans have taken the opportunity to memorialize him. Several counties, municipalities, streets, public schools, and universities are named after him. Philadelphia, where Franklin spent much of his life, is home to the Benjamin Franklin

The United States' largest banknote, the $100 bill, features a picture of Benjamin Franklin on one side and an image of Independence Hall on the other.

Bridge and Ben Franklin Parkway. Boston has Franklin Park, including a zoo and a conservatory. There's even a crater on the moon named after him! Philadelphia also houses the Franklin Institute, a science museum and research center founded in 1824, making it one of the oldest such centers of science in the country. Inside the institute, one can visit the Benjamin Franklin National Memorial, a 20-foot- (6.1 m) tall statue of Franklin carved out of marble. It was made in the early 1900s. Governed by the National Park Service, the memorial sees over one hundred thousand visitors each year.

Benjamin Franklin Today

All of that pomp and circumstance around Benjamin Franklin's memory isn't just fluff—it's there to remind us of the impact that Franklin's life had on the world around him, as well as the impact he continues to have on those living in the US today.

Without Franklin, our founding documents might look very different indeed. One example of Franklin's hand in the Declaration of Independence are the three words he physically crossed out on one of the "rough draft" versions of the declaration, which one can view in the Library of Congress. Using heavy backslashes, Franklin crossed out the last three words of the phrase "We hold these truths to be sacred and undeniable," written by Jefferson, and replaced it with those that we all now know: "We hold these truths to be self-evident."[1] This change might seem small, but the use of the word "sacred" asserted that the truths in question were an assertion of emotion and religion. Franklin's edit turned the phrase into an assertion of rationality and reason, potentially even subject to revision. It was changes like this one that made Franklin's seat at the table an invaluable one.

Of course, Franklin's seat at the writing table for the founding documents never would have existed if not for the role he played in bringing the American Revolution to fruition. His diplomacy in France, which caused the country to loan the colonists large sums of money to fund the war, was necessary if the colonists were to gain America's independence. Franklin's leadership, communication, and fundraising skills were unmatched in early America, making him an extremely worthwhile piece of the revolutionary puzzle. Without him, the process may have been much slower, or more painful, or simply less successful. It is hard to say where the United States would be without Benjamin Franklin—or if it would *be* at all.

The original drafts of the Declaration of Independence were written by hand and include numerous comments, cross-outs, and corrections by each of the "Committee of Five."

Franklin also took care to ensure that he would be remembered fondly. Before his death, he bequeathed a total of £2,000 (equivalent to about $35,000 in 2018) to the cities of Boston and Philadelphia, and made sure that most of the money could not be drawn on for one hundred years. For the rest, the cities would have to wait two hundred years. He requested that the money be divided equally between Philadelphia and Boston to be used as loans for young apprentices, just as he himself had once been. Today, the remaining funds in Franklin's bequest are worth $6.5 million. Franklin set the money aside while he worked as governor of Pennsylvania in the last years of his life,

The Benjamin Franklin Bridge, one of many places and things named after the Founding Father, connects the cities of Philadelphia, Pennsylvania, and Camden, New Jersey, over the Delaware River.

from 1785 to 1788. He firmly believed that public servants should not be paid, and had personally wished that the rule be written into law. The cities of Philadelphia and Boston, as well as their home states of Pennsylvania and Massachusetts, who also received portions of the bequest, are still in talks about how, exactly, the funds should be spent. It may be many more years before we see the final results of Franklin's eighteenth-century generosity at work in our twenty-first-century world.

Myths and Stories

For all of Franklin's popularity, and for all of the heavily researched biographies that have been written about him, including his own memoirs, misconceptions and myths about the man still remain. One of the silliest Franklin stories centers around the idea that Benjamin Franklin wanted the United States' national bird to be the turkey. Franklin did write a letter to his daughter criticizing the eagle design for the Great Seal. He bad-mouthed the bird itself, writing, "For my own part I wish the Bald Eagle had not been chosen the Representative of our Country. He is a Bird of bad moral Character. He does not get his Living honestly. You may have seen him perched on some dead Tree near the River, where, too lazy to fish for himself, he watches the Labour of the Fishing Hawk; and when that diligent Bird has at length taken a Fish, and is bearing it to his Nest for the Support of his Mate and young Ones, the Bald Eagle pursues him and takes it from him." He then goes on to say, "I am on this account not displeased that the Figure is not known as a Bald Eagle, but looks more like a Turkey. For the Truth the Turkey is in Comparison a much more respectable Bird, and withal a true original Native of America … He is besides, though a little vain & silly, a Bird of Courage."[2] Franklin certainly defended the turkey's honor in comparison

FRANKLIN'S WORDS

One of Franklin's most memorable contributions to early American life was his wit and wisdom, most often put on display in *Poor Richard's Almanack*. While some, like Mark Twain, took issue with the little virtues suggested by the writer, the general population embraced his proverbs, turning them into well-known, often-repeated snippets, though many who repeat the words today may not realize that they originated with Benjamin Franklin. The following are some of his most popular sayings, all from *Poor Richard's Almanack*:

"Love your Enemies, for they tell you your faults."
"Better slip with foot than tongue."
"A true Friend is the best Possession."
"No gains without pains."
"What you seem to be, be really."
"When you're good to others, you're best to yourself."[3]

Poor Richard, 1744.

AN

Almanack

For the Year of Chrift

1744,

It being LEAP-YEAR,

And makes fince the Creation	Years
By the Account of the Eaftern *Greeks*	7252
By the Latin Church, when ☉ ent. ♈	6943
By the Computation of *W. W.*	5753
By the *Roman* Chronology	5693
By the *Jewifh* Rabbies	5505

Wherein is contained,

The Lunations, Eclipfes, Judgment of the Weather, Spring Tides, Planets Motions & mutual Afpects, Sun and Moon's Rifing and Setting, Length of Days, Time of High Water, Fairs, Courts, and obfervable Days.

Fitted to the Latitude of Forty Degrees, and a Meridian of Five Hours Weft from *London*, but may without fenfible Error, ferve all the adjacent Places, even from *Newfoundland* to *South-Carolina.*

By *RICHARD SAUNDERS,* Philom.

PHILADELPHIA:
Printed and fold by B. *FRANKLIN.* Sold also by *JONAS GREEN,* at *Annapolis.*

Some think of *Poor Richard's Almanack* as Franklin's greatest business accomplishment, as his book was published every year over a twenty-five-year period, starting in 1732.

to the rascal bald eagle, but he did not propose that it become the national bird. On that subject, he was rather silent.

Another popular myth is that Franklin is the father of daylight saving time, the practice of moving the clock forward one hour in the spring. In 1784, Franklin penned a satirical essay, titled "An Economical Project." In that essay, he writes of the benefits of natural daylight over candles and oil lamps. He wrote, "An immense sum! That the city of Paris might save every year, by the economy of using sunshine instead of candles."[4] He went on to give tongue-in-cheek regulations that would help Parisians wake early each morning, none of which included daylight saving time. In truth, the idea wasn't presented until 1895, when a New Zealand entomologist named George Hudson suggested that additional daylight would be beneficial, especially for his hobby of insect collecting.

Franklin said and wrote many wise things. His letters and almanacs were full of useful sayings, including business advice that helped give a head start to wealth creation in the young nation. Today, many remember Franklin as the originator of the phrase "a penny saved is a penny earned," but Franklin never said it! In a later edition of his almanac, he wrote, "A penny saved is two pence clear."[5]

Enduring Legacy

In the twenty-first century, we may not own glass armonicas, flip through the pages of our almanacs each day, or think deeply about lightning rods attached to the church steeples in town. However, all the same, Benjamin Franklin left his mark on the lives of all Americans who enjoy life and liberty in the United States today. His leadership and diplomacy ensured that the colonies wouldn't stay the colonies forever, but would find their footing as an independent democracy, built with steady hands on strong founding documents, in no small part due to Franklin's careful oversight. His keen intellect and passionate curiosity were the catalyst for many practical innovations, and his general determination and writing ability led to some of the most enduring works to come out of eighteenth-century America. Though Franklin was a flawed man, he always strove for virtue. That striving alone is one of the "American values" that many see in Benjamin Franklin, and, if nothing else, the push to improve oneself is certainly a character trait worth emulating.

CHRONOLOGY

1706 Benjmin Franklin is born on January 17 in Boston, Massachusetts.

1722 Franklin's first essay is published, at the age of sixteen, under the pen name Silence Dogood.

1723 Franklin moves to Philadelphia.

1727 The Junto group is established in Philadelphia. Franklin is a founding member.

1728 Franklin opens his very own print shop. In 1729, he begins to publish from the shop his very first newspaper, the *Pennsylvania Gazette*.

1730 Franklin and Deborah Read Rogers become common-law husband and wife. Franklin's son William is born to another woman.

1732 Deborah gives birth to their first son, Francis, and Franklin releases the first publication of his almanac.

1736 Franklin forms the Union Fire Company, Philadelphia's first brigade.

1736 Franklin's son Francis dies of smallpox at age four.

1742 Franklin invents a new type of stove.

1744 Deborah gives birth to their daughter, Sarah, in September.

1748 Franklin officially retires from printing.

1752 Franklin conducts his famous kite-flying experiment.

1754 French and Indian War begins and Franklin works to unite the colonies.

1757 Franklin travels to England to work on behalf of the colonies. Franklin would live there for eighteen years.

1762 Franklin invents the glass armonica.

1774 Deborah Franklin dies.

1775 The Revolutionary War begins.

1776 The American colonies declare their independence from Britain.

1783 Franklin signs the Treaty of Paris in France, officially ending the American Revolutionary war.

1787 Franklin assists in writing the US Constitution.

1790 Franklin dies at home in Philadelphia, Pennsylvania, at the age of eighty-four.

1793 The first English edition of Franklin's autobiography is published.

1865 Slavery officially ends in the United States with the ratification of the Thirteenth Amendment to the Constitution.

GLOSSARY

abolition The movement to end slavery.

almanac An annual publication that includes weather forecasts, moon phases, agricultural dates, tide tables, and more.

American Revolution A conflict that took place between 1765 and 1783, coalescing around tensions between the thirteen colonies and Great Britain.

apprentice A person who agrees to work for a fixed period of time in order to learn from a skilled tradesman.

autobiography A self-written account of one's own life.

bifocals A type of eyeglasses that contain two lens powers.

colony A region under full or partial control of another country and occupied by settlers from that distant country.

common-law marriage An informal marriage, in which a couple is considered married even though they have not formally registered their union with the state.

Continental Congress The governing body of the thirteen colonies during the American Revolution. It first met to organize resistance to Parliament's Coercive Acts.

Declaration of Independence The official resolution, adopted on July 4, 1776, that declared the thirteen colonies were at war with Great Britain and now regarded themselves as free and independent.

diplomat A person selected by the state to represent his or her country while abroad.

Founding Father Seven key figures who spearheaded the American Revolution and helped to establish the governmental foundation of the United States of America.

Franklin stove A cast-iron stove, invented by Benjamin Franklin in 1742, that is used to heat a room.

friction machine A type of machine, popular in the eighteenth century, that generated static electricity by direct physical contact.

Gulf Stream A warm and quickly moving current in the Atlantic Ocean.

inter To bury someone.

Junto Also known as the Leather Apron Club, a group established by Benjamin Franklin in 1727 for the purpose of discussion, debate, and improvement.

lightning rod A metal rod attached to the top of a building or tall structure in order to attract lightning and direct it into the ground.

Loyalist One who remained loyal to British control during the American Revolution.

New World A name for the Americas that was used during colonization by the Europeans.

odometer A tool that measures the distance traveled.

patriot A colonist who rebelled against British control during the American Revolution.

pleuritic Describing an inflammation of the tissue lining the lungs and chest.

political cartoon A drawing that contains commentary expressing the artist's opinion about its political subjects.

proverb A simple saying that states a truth or offers a piece of advice.

ratification Formal approval or consent to a contract, treaty, or agreement.

revolutionary Causing a dramatic change.

semaphore A system in which messages are sent across distances using towers and signals on poles, flags, or different arm movements.

smallpox A contagious and often deadly disease that was eradicated worldwide by 1980.

Stamp Act An official motion by the British Parliament, enacted in 1765, that taxed the American colonies by requiring printed materials to be produced on stamped paper from London.

treaty A formal agreement between international governments.

Treaty of Paris A document, negotiated between the United States and Great Britain, that ended the Revolutionary War and recognized American independence.

US Constitution The founding document and supreme law of the United States that sets out the framework for the federal government through seven distinct articles.

virtue A quality, behavior, or power that shows high moral standards.

SOURCES

CHAPTER ONE

1. US Census Bureau, *Bicentennial Edition: Historical Statistics of the United States, Colonial Times to 1970*, Washington, DC, 1975.

2. Darold D. Wax, "The Demand for Slave Labor in Colonial Pennsylvania," *Pennsylvania History: A Journal of Mid-Atlantic Studies* Vol. 34, No. 4. University Park, PA: Penn State University Press, 1967, http://www.jstor.org/stable/27770523.

3. Albert G. MacKey, *Encyclopedia of Freemasonry 1909*, The Masonic History Company, 2003.

4. Great Britain, Parliament, *House of Commons, The examination of doctor Benjamin Franklin, before an august assembly [the House of commons] relating to the repeal of the Stamp-act, &c*, 1766.

5. Ibid.

6. *Boston, December 20, on Tuesday last the body of the people of this and all the adjacent towns, an others from the distance of twenty miles, assembled at the old south meeting house to inquire the reason of the delay in sending the ship Dartmout*, Boston, MA, 1773, Retrieved from the Library of Congress, Accessed February 26, 2018, https://www.loc.gov/item/rbpe.0370250a.

7. Adam Smith, 1723–1790, *The Wealth of Nations / Adam Smith; Introduction by Robert Reich*; Edited, with Notes, Marginal Summary, and Enlarged Index by Edwin Cannan, New York: Modern Library, 2000.

CHAPTER TWO

1. "From Benjamin Franklin to Deborah Franklin, 6 January 1773," *Founders Online*, National Archives, last modified February 1, 2018, http://founders.archives.gov/documents/Franklin/01-20-02-0010.

2. Benjamin Franklin, *Autobiography of Benjamin Franklin*, Norton Critical Edition, ed. Joyce E. Chaplin (New York: W. W. Norton, 2012).

3. Ibid.

4. "Silence Dogood, No. 1, 2 April 1722," *Founders Online*, National Archives, February 1, 2018, http://founders.archives.gov/documents/Franklin/01-01-02-0008.

5. Benjamin Franklin, *Autobiography of Benjamin Franklin*, Norton Critical Edition, ed. Joyce E. Chaplin (New York: W. W. Norton, 2012).

6. "Plan of Conduct, 1726," *Founders Online*, National Archives, February 1, 2018, http://founders.archives.gov/documents/Franklin/01-01-02-0030.

7. "Last Will and Testament, 28 April 1757," *Founders Online*, National Archives, February 1, 2018, http://founders.archives.gov/documents/Franklin/01-07-02-0085.

8. Benjamin Franklin, *Autobiography of Benjamin Franklin*, Norton Critical Edition, ed. Joyce E. Chaplin (New York: W. W. Norton, 2012).

9. Ibid.

10. "Epitaph, 1728," *Founders Online*, National Archives, February 1, 2018, http://founders.archives.gov/documents/Franklin/01-01-02-0033.

CHAPTER THREE

1. "From Thomas Jefferson to Ferdinand Grand, 23 April 1790," *Founders Online*, National Archives. February 1, 2018, http://founders.archives.gov/documents/Jefferson/01-16-02-0208.

2. "III. Thomas Jefferson to the Rev. William Smith, 19 February 1791," *Founders Online*, National Archives, February 1, 2018, http://founders.archives.gov/documents/Jefferson/01-19-02-0005-0009.

3. "To Thomas Jefferson from Benjamin Franklin, 20 March 1786," *Founders Online*, National Archives, last modified February 1, 2018, http://founders.archives.gov/documents/Jefferson/01-09-02-0308.

4. "From George Washington to Benjamin Franklin, 23 September 1789," *Founders Online*, National Archives, last modified February 1, 2018, http://founders.archives.gov/documents/Washington/05-04-02-0045.

5. "From John Adams to Benjamin Rush, 4 April 1790," *Founders Online,* National Archives, last modified February 1, 2018, http://founders.archives.gov/documents/ Adams/99-02-02-0903.

6. Benjamin Franklin, *Autobiography of Benjamin Franklin,* Norton Critical Edition, ed. Joyce E. Chaplin (New York: W. W. Norton, 2012).

7. "Benjamin Franklin to William Franklin," August 16, 1784, Albert Henry Smith, ed., *The Writings of Benjamin Franklin,* New York, 1906.

8. Ibid.

CHAPTER FOUR

1. "From Benjamin Franklin to Peter Collinson, 25 May 1747," *Founders Online*, National Archives, February 1, 2018, http://founders.archives.gov/documents/ Franklin/01-03-02-0059.

2. "Opinions and Conjectures, [29 July 1750]," *Founders Online,* National Archives, last modified February 1, 2018, http://founders.archives.gov/documents/ Franklin/01-04-02-0006.

3. "To George Whatley, 21 August 1784," franklinpapers. org, http://franklinpapers.org/franklin/framedVolumes. jsp?vol=42&page=147.

4. Benjamin Franklin, *Autobiography of Benjamin Franklin*, Norton Critical Edition, ed. Joyce E. Chaplin (New York: W. W. Norton, 2012).

5. Ibid.

CHAPTER FIVE

1. Paul Leicester Ford, *The Many-Sided Franklin* (New York: The Century Co., 1899).

2. Mark Twain, *The Writings of Mark Twain Volume 19* (Hartford, CT: American Publishing Company, 1899).

3. Mark Twain, "Letter From Mark Twain: A First Visit to Boston," *San Francisco Alta California*, July 1869.

4. D. H. Lawrence, *Studies in Classic American Literature* (New York: Thomas Seltzer, 1923).

5. Ibid.

6. "Madison Debates, [17 September 1787]," *The Avalon Project*, Lillian Goldman Law Library, 2008, http://avalon.law.yale.edu/18th_century/debates_917.asp#1.

CHAPTER SIX

1. *The Papers of Thomas Jefferson*, Vol. 1, 1760–1776, ed. Julian P. Boyd (Princeton, NJ: Princeton University Press, 1950), 243–247.

2. "To Sarah Bache, 26 January 1784," franklinpapers. org, http://franklinpapers.org/franklin/framedVolumes. jsp?vol=41&page=281.

3. "Poor Richard Improved, 1756," *Founders Online*, National Archives, February 1, 2018, http://founders.archives.gov/ documents/Franklin/01-06-02-0136.

4. "To the Authors of The Journal of Paris," 1784, "Images of Benjamin Franklin: As Seen by Himself and Others," Mamdouha S. Bobst Gallery, Bobst Library, New York University, 2006, https://commons.wikimedia.org/wiki/ File:Franklin-Benjamin-Journal-de-Paris-1784.png.

5. "Poor Richard, 1737," *Founders Online*, National Archives, February 1, 2018, http://founders.archives.gov/documents/ Franklin/01-02-02-0028.

FURTHER INFORMATION

BOOKS

Eighmey, Rae Katherine. *Stirring the Pot with Benjamin Franklin: A Founding Father's Culinary Adventures.* Washington, DC: Smithsonian Books, 2018.

Fleming, Thomas. *Ben Franklin: Inventing America.* Minneapolis, MN: Voyageur Press, 2016.

Quirk, Anne. *The Good Fight: The Feuds of the Founding Fathers (And How They Shaped the Nation).* New York: Knopf Books for Young Readers, 2017.

Rockliff, Mara. *Mesmerized: How Ben Franklin Solved a Mystery That Baffled All of France.* Somerville, MA: Candlewick Press, 2017.

Thompson, Ben. *Guts & Glory: The American Revolution.* New York: Little, Brown Books for Education, 2017.

WEBSITES

America's Story from America's Library: Benjamin Franklin
http://www.americaslibrary.gov/aa/franklinb/aa_franklinb_
subj.html

This site includes stories about Benjamin Franklin's life, as well as a timeline. Here you can also hear and learn about other amazing Americans.

11 Surprising Facts About Benjamin Franklin
http://www.history.com/news/11-surprising-facts-about-
benjamin-franklin

Fun and surprising facts are listed on this site. There are also pictures and links to other historical facts and stories.

PBS: Benjamin Franklin
http://www.pbs.org/benfranklin/index.html

On this page, you can explore countless aspects of Benjamin Franklin's life, search through a detailed timeline, and even get the scoop on Franklin "A to Z."

ORGANIZATIONS

Franklin and Marshall College
415 Harrisburg Ave, Lancaster, PA 17603

The Franklin Institute
222 N 20th St, Philadelphia, PA 19103

The Museum of the American Revolution
101 S 3rd St, Philadelphia, PA 19106

BIBLIOGRAPHY

Anderson, AnnMarie. *Benjamin Franklin*. New York: Scholastic Inc., 2014.

Andrews, Evan. "11 Surprising Facts About Benjamin Franklin." History. January 15, 2016. http://www.history.com/news/11-surprising-facts-about-benjamin-franklin.

Butterfield, Fox. "From Ben Franklin, a Gift That's Worth Two Fights." *New York Times*. April 21, 1990. http://www.nytimes.com/1990/04/21/us/from-ben-franklin-a-gift-that-s-worth-two-fights.html.

Byrd, Robert. *Electric Ben: The Amazing Life and Times of Benjamin Franklin*. New York: Dial Book for Young Readers/Penguin Group, 2012.

Crawford, Laura. *Benjamin Franklin From A to Z*. Gretna, LA: Pelican Publishing Company, 2013.

"Epitaph, 1728." *Founders Online*, National Archives. February 1, 2018. https://founders.archives.gov/documents/Franklin/01-01-02-0033.

Eschner, Kat. "Benjamin Franklin Was the First to Chart the Gulf Stream." Smithsonian. May 2, 2017. https://www.smithsonianmag.com/smart-news/benjamin-franklin-was-first-chart-gulf-stream-180963066.

Folsom, Burton, and Blaine McCormick. "A Penny Saved
    Was Never a Penny Earned." *Forbes.* August 18, 2014.
    https://www.forbes.com/sites/realspin/2014/08/18/a-
    penny-saved-was-never-a-penny-earned/#6d4bff382e88.

Fleming, Thomas. *Ben Franklin: Inventing America.*
    Minneapolis, MN: Voyageur Press, 2016.

Franklin, Benjamin. *Autobiography of Benjamin Franklin.*
    New York: W. W. Norton, 2012.

Freedman, Russell. *Becoming Ben Franklin: How a Candle-
    Maker's Son Helped Light the Flame of Liberty.* New York:
    Holiday House, 2013.

Goodwin, George. *Benjamin Franklin in London: The British
    Life of America's Founding Father.* New Haven, CT:
    Yale University Press, 2017.

Great Britain. Parliament. *House of Commons. The Examination
    of Doctor Benjamin Franklin, Before an August Assembly [the
    House of Commons] Relating to the Repeal of the Stamp-Act,
    &c.* 1766.

Michie, Thomas Johnson, Thomas Jefferson, and Peachy R.
    Grattan. *Virginia Reports: Jefferson–33 Grattan, 1730–
    1880.* Charlottesville, VA: The Michie Co.

Kidd, Thomas S. "How Benjamin Franklin, a Deist, Became
    the Founding Father of a Unique Kind of American
    Faith." *Washington Post.* June 28, 2017. https://www.
    washingtonpost.com/news/acts-of-faith/wp/2017/06/28/

how-benjamin-franklin-a-deist-became-the-founding-
father-of-a-unique-kind-of-american-faith/?utm_term=.
d782cf4cee17.

Lacayo, Richard. *Benjamin Franklin: An Illustrated History of
His Life and Times.* New York: Time, Inc., 2010.

Leavitt, Amie Jane. *Who Really Discovered Electricity?*
Mankato, MN: Capstone Press, 2011.

Lopez, Claude-Anne. "Why He Was a Babe Magnet." *Time.*
July 7, 2003. http://content.time.com/time/magazine/
article/0,9171,1005155-3,00.html.

Lossing, Benson John. *Harpers' Popular Cyclopaedia of
United States History from the Aboriginal Period to
1876: Containing Brief Sketches of Important Events and
Conspicuous Actors, Volume 2.* New York: Harper, 1881.

Mara, Wil. *Benjamin Franklin.* New York: Children's Press,
2015.

Middlekauff, Robert. *Benjamin Franklin and His Enemies.*
Oakland, CA: University of California Press, 1998.

Nelson, Maria. *Famous Lives: The Life of Ben Franklin.*
New York: Gareth Stevens Publishing, 2012.

"Old Mistresses Apologue, 25 June 1745." *Founders Online.*
National Archives. http://founders.archives.gov/
documents/Franklin/01-03-02-0011.

"Plan of Conduct, 1726." *Founders Online*. National Archives. February 1, 2018. http://founders.archives.gov/documents/ Franklin/01-01-02-0030.

Quirk, Anne. *The Good Fight: The Feuds of the Founding Fathers (And How They Shaped the Nation)*. New York: Knopf Books for Young Readers, 2017.

Rockliff, Mara. *Mesmerized: How Ben Franklin Solved a Mystery That Baffled All of France*. Somerville, MA: Candlewick Press, 2017.

Sachse, Julius F. "The Masonic Chronology of Benjamin Franklin." *Pennsylvania Magazine of History and Biography*. 1906. http://www.jstor.org/stable/20085334.

Seybold, Matt. "The Best Defense is a Good Offense: False Virtue, Fake News, & Mark Twain's Birthday Roast of Ben Franklin." Center for Mark Twain Studies. January 17, 2017. http://marktwainstudies.com/the-best-defense-is-a-good-offense-false-virtue-fake-news-mark-twains-birthday-roast-of-ben-franklin.

"Silence Dogood, No. 1, 2 April 1722." *Founders Online*. National Archives. http://founders.archives.gov/ documents/Franklin/01-01-02-0008.

Skemp, Sheila L. "My Son, My Enemy." *Time*. July 7, 2003. http://content.time.com/time/magazine/article /0,9171,1005156,00.html.

Thompson, Ben. *Guts & Glory: The American Revolution*. New York: Little, Brown Books for Education, 2017.

Twain, Mark. *The Writings of Mark Twain Volume 19*. Hartford, CT: American Publishing Company, 1899.

US Census Bureau. *Bicentennial Edition: Historical Statistics of the United States, Colonial Times to 1970*. Washington, DC, 1975.

INDEX

ABOUT THE AUTHOR

Kaitlyn Duling believes in the power of words to change hearts, minds, and, ultimately, actions. A writer who grew up in Illinois, she now resides in Pittsburgh, Pennsylvania, where she has written over thirty books for children. She knows that knowledge of the past is the key to our future, and wants to make sure that all children and families have access to high-quality information.